INDIA 2014

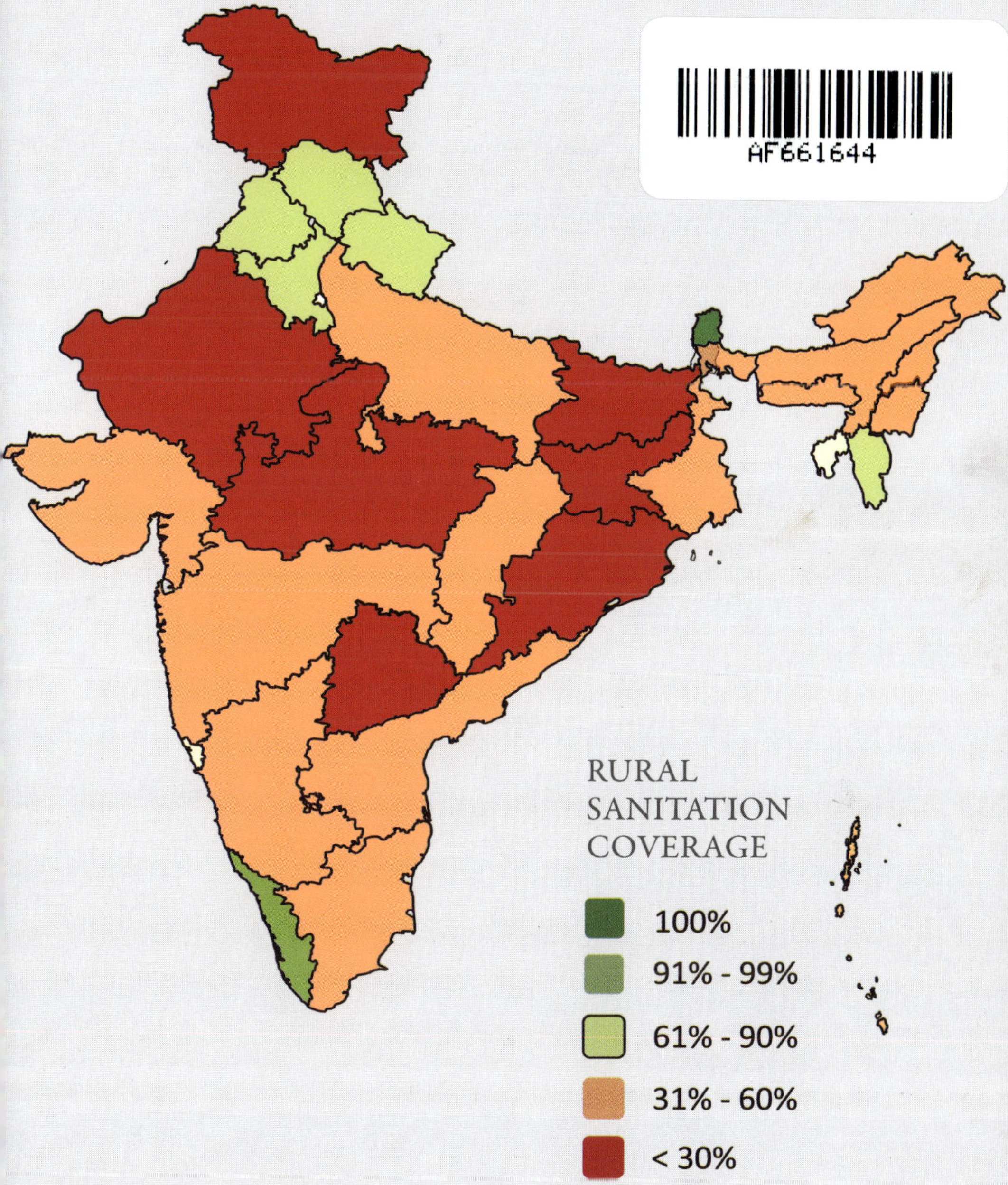

THE SWACHH BHARAT REVOLUTION

Advance Praise for *The Swachh Bharat Revolution*

'It is a rare occurrence in history that a public health programme captures the imagination of over a billion people. The stories shared by the variety of stakeholders in this book – from policymakers to policy implementers to development partners to celebrities to grassroots sanitation champions – are proof that this Mission truly went way beyond a typical government scheme and became the shared vision of a nation.'

– **Soumya Swaminathan**, Deputy Director-General of Programmes, World Health Organization

'The way the people of this great nation responded to the Prime Minister's clarion call of ending open defecation in under five years is testament to the fact that when the collective force of over a billion people is effectively channelized, nothing is impossible. If Bapu were here with us today, he would be proud not only of what we have achieved, but also the way we have achieved it. This book is a true reflection of that indomitable spirit which has transformed the Swachh Bharat Mission into the largest mass movement in independent India.'

– **Smriti Zubin Irani**, Cabinet Minister, Government of India

'Seldom has a government programme, anywhere in the world, transformed into a people's movement like the Swachh Bharat Mission has. I consider myself fortunate to have played my part in it. This book is a testament to the success of this iconic mission, as well as a recipe for creating a social revolution.'

– **Amitabh Bachchan**, Actor and Swachh Bharat Ambassador

THE SWACHH BHARAT REVOLUTION

FOUR PILLARS OF INDIA'S BEHAVIOURAL TRANSFORMATION

EDITED BY PARAMESWARAN IYER

HarperCollins *Publishers* India

First published in hardback in India in 2019 by
HarperCollins *Publishers*
A-75, Sector 57, Noida, Uttar Pradesh 201301, India
www.harpercollins.co.in

2 4 6 8 10 9 7 5 3 1

P-ISBN: 978-93-5357-267-9
E-ISBN: 978-93-5357-268-6

Typeset in 11/15 Sabon LT Std at
Manipal Digital Systems, Manipal

Printed and bound at
Thomson Press (India) Ltd

MIX
Paper
FSC FSC® C010615

This book is produced from independently certified FSC® paper to ensure responsible forest management.

To the people of India and the hundreds of thousands of swachhagrahis who made the revolution possible

Contents

PEOPLE'S PARTICIPATION

Foreword
Ek Kadam Swachhata Ki Ore

NARENDRA MODI

Prime Minister of India

THERE WERE TWO things extremely close to Mahatma Gandhi's heart – the independence of India, and sanitation. But, given a choice between these two, he said that for him, sanitation was even more important than political independence. India won political independence during his lifetime, on 15 August 1947. But his dream of a Clean India remained unfulfilled even decades after his passing. Rural sanitation coverage, for instance, was still at a mere 38 per cent even in 2014, when our Government first assumed office. This is nearly seven decades since Independence and after three decades of Government-managed sanitation campaigns and programmes. Clearly, something needed to change if we were ever to realize Bapu's dream.

When it was time to make my maiden Independence Day address from the ramparts of the Red Fort on 15 August 2014, it was an opportunity to bring to the forefront of public discourse the issue of Swachhata – particularly the national shame of open defecation. This was seen as an unprecedented move because few in our country even acknowledged the existence of this problem. The fact that 60 crore Indians still defecated in the open every day pained me, especially the fact that our mothers and sisters had to wait till dark to relieve themselves and be exposed to various diseases.

We cannot solve what we cannot address. So, a key part of that Independence Day address was the announcement of the Swachh Bharat Mission. I asked all Indians if we do not owe it to Mahatma Gandhi for our village, our city, our street, our community, our school, our temple, our hospital, and all areas around us to become free from dirt and filth. We gave ourselves a target of ending open defecation forever and fulfilling Bapu's dream of a Swachh Bharat by 2 October 2019, his 150th birth anniversary.

This was never a goal to be achieved as a Government programme only. Swachhata had to be taken up as a collective national responsibility by every citizen of India. If we all came together and joined hands to make it a people's movement, then there was no reason why we would not be counted among the cleanest nations of the world. This endeavour was beyond politics. We needed to undertake this work motivated by our patriotism and nationalism, free from the influence of politics. This movement was important for the health of the poor, the health of our children, the health of the weakest in our society. And that is what made it a true nationalistic endeavour.

Today, as we stand in the year 2019, it is a matter of pride that the progress made by this Mission has proved that with commitment, even the most impossible-looking task can be made possible if we all work together. It is a true example of the resilience and grit of the people of this country. These last few years, I have had the privilege of meeting and hearing of some incredible and inspiring swachhata warriors from across the country. From Kashmir to Kanyakumari, and Kutch to Kohima, we have all heard stories of swachhata champions who went above and beyond the call of duty to make Swachh Bharat a reality.

Everyone associated with this movement is a swachhagrahi. Swachhagrahis embody the ideas and ideals of Gandhiji and have provided a new momentum, a new energy and a new life to moving from Satyagraha to Swachhagraha. In the future too, whenever anything is written about this movement, the names of India's swachhagrahis will be taken with reverence, much like that of the freedom fighters of India's Satyagraha. Just as the satyagrahis led India to political freedom, the swachhagrahis are leading India to freedom from open defecation.

Gram pradhans and sarpanchs have also played a key role in this movement. At the outset of the Mission, pradhans of Ganga bank villages took an oath that they will ensure that the practice of open defecation is ended in all their villages and ensure that the river is not polluted by them. All Ganga bank villages were declared Open Defecation Free almost two years before the rest of the nation!

The media of this country also deserves a special mention. They helped keep the government accountable, mobilized citizens' movements, and led local cleanliness-related initiatives out of their own corporate social responsibility. The nation congratulates them for this historic contribution which has proven that the media too can play an active and positive role in meeting the developmental goals of the nation.

This book is a sincere effort to encompass the various aspects of this programme – as a people's movement, as a government scheme, as an economic revolution, as a sanitation revolution. My gratitude to all the authors who have taken time to contribute to this book and helped chronicle this multi-faceted Mission from their perspective.

It is to be reiterated that Bapu's dream of a Clean India became achievable only when 130 crore Indians came together and made it happen. I hope this book will show the rest of the world that amazing things can be achieved when people unite for a cause. India's sanitation revolution will continue to inspire the world to end global open defecation forever.

नरेन्द्र मोदी

Preface

GAJENDRA SINGH SHEKHAWAT

Union Minister for Jal Shakti, Government of India

THE SWACHH BHARAT Mission is much more than a Government programme, or a sanitation programme. Over the past five years, India has seen a social revolution – a movement, of the people, by the people and for the people. The people of India rallied behind the clarion call of their Prime Minister, and collectively changed habits that they had held on to for centuries. This has transformed the sanitation narrative in India and has the potential of doing so throughout the world. It is a fascinating story that must be told.

Several ancient Indian scriptures talk about the importance of sanitation and cleanliness for a healthy body and mind. In fact, the first advanced networked sanitation systems in the world were developed in the Indus valley civilization. Over the years, our focus on sanitation had dwindled, until the day Prime Minister Modi put sanitation back fairly and squarely on the national agenda. And, as they say, the rest is history. From a sanitation coverage base of just 39 per cent in 2014, India is now on the verge of becoming open defecation free. And this transformation has had a significant impact on the lives of our people, especially our mothers, sisters and daughters.

While India has achieved tremendous results on swachhata, we must not and will not rest on our laurels. Sustaining the gains we have achieved will remain a key priority of the Government. And going forward, in the next phase of the Swachh Bharat Mission, we will strive to achieve 100 per cent solid and liquid waste management. Along with this very important goal, we are working towards ensuring piped water supply for all households in India by adopting a similar approach as we did in the Swachh Bharat Mission: making it a jan andolan, a people's movement.

The Swachh Bharat Mission has been an embodiment of the collective spirit of a nation, showing that with a strong and committed political leadership, public financing, partnerships and most importantly people's participation in the developmental process, no goal is too difficult to achieve. It has set forth a framework for other large-scale social transformation initiatives in India and the world. This book attempts to capture this fascinating story through the lens of many of its architects.

I hope this inspires readers around the world to attempt to bring about change for the better in their communities and gives them a glimpse into one of the largest behaviour change campaigns in the world.

Jai Hind.

Introduction

PARAMESWARAN IYER

Secretary, Department of Drinking Water and Sanitation,
Ministry of Jal Shakti, Government of India

WHEN THE NEWLY elected Prime Minister of India, Narendra Modi, commenced his maiden Independence Day speech on 15 August 2014, my wife, Indira, and I were curious about his vision for the nation and the development agenda going forward. We were then living in Hanoi, Vietnam, where I was working for the World Bank. Forty-five minutes into his speech, we were jolted into amazement: the Prime Minister, in his first major address to the nation, was talking about the lack of toilets and the indignity of women and girls having to defecate in the open. This was unheard of; something culturally and socially taboo in most countries, especially in India, where such a topic was not discussed in polite society, let alone during a Prime Ministerial address to the nation.

The Prime Minister went on to announce that India would launch a Swachh Bharat Mission (SBM) – the Clean India Mission – and as a tribute to the Father of the Nation, rid the country of open defecation by 2 October 2019, the 150th birth anniversary of the Mahatma. I was beside myself with excitement and recall saying to my wife: 'I've somehow got to get back to India and be a part of this programme. This is a once-in-a-lifetime opportunity to rid our country of open defecation.' It was a very long shot, since I had left the Indian Administrative Service in 2009 and joined World Bank. Fortunately for me, however, about a year later, I was sounded out about my interest in returning to India and, in February 2016, was appointed Secretary to the Government of India in the Ministry of Drinking Water and Sanitation,[1] the nodal ministry for the Swachh Bharat Mission.

As I write this, it has been less than five years after the Prime Minister's audacious announcement from the Red Fort. Flying in the face of naysayers who said that it was impossible to achieve Open Defecation Free (ODF) status in only five years, SBM, under the leadership of Prime Minister Modi, has increased India's rural sanitation coverage to 99 per cent. We are now fully on track to achieve the goal of ridding the country of open defecation before the deadline of 2 October 2019.

Achieving an ODF India in record time also means that India is attaining Sustainable Development Goal (SDG) 6.2 – Sanitation for all – a whopping eleven years before the UN's SDG target of 31 December 2030. From having the dubious distinction of being the home of 60 crore people practising open defecation in 2014 – 60 per cent of the world's total population of open defecators – to achieving ODF status through behaviour change at scale, in less than five years, is nothing short of a miracle. Inspired and led by the Prime Minister, however, the country and its billion-plus population have done it. Impossible is indeed nothing!

Few would dispute that SBM today has become Indian's sanitation revolution and one of the biggest behaviour change mass movements in history. The scale of the achievement, especially in rural India, is mind boggling. As the graph below indicates, the low rural sanitation

---

1 Now Department of Drinking Water and Sanitation, Ministry of Jal Shakti

coverage in India at the start of SBM meant that there were only about 7 crore individual household latrines (IHHLs) in rural India at the time. As of June 2019, almost 9.7 crore new toilets have been added, ensuring that virtually all rural households in India have access to a toilet at home, and sanitation coverage has increased from 39 per cent to over 99 per cent in these five years.

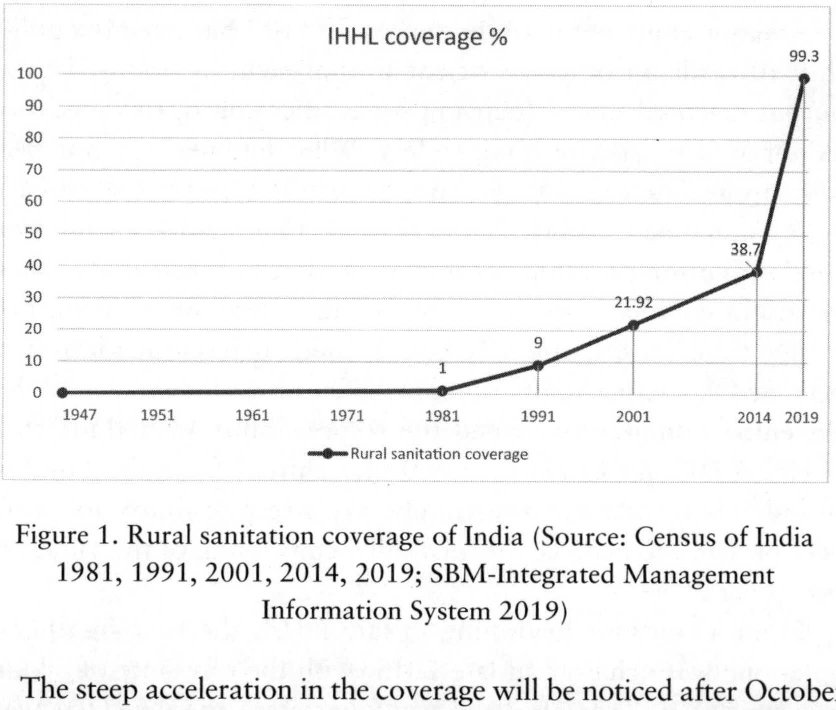

Figure 1. Rural sanitation coverage of India (Source: Census of India 1981, 1991, 2001, 2014, 2019; SBM-Integrated Management Information System 2019)

The steep acceleration in the coverage will be noticed after October 2014, with the slope taking a rocket-like trajectory towards the end. The numbers are quite staggering: over 5,67,489 villages have become ODF as of June 2019. Most importantly, the usage of toilets, the best indicator of behaviour change, is very high, estimated at well over 95 per cent by the World Bank Support Project's Independent Verification Agency through its most recent National Annual Rural Sanitation Survey (NARSS) in 6,136 villages and 92,040 households across all states of India (March 2019).

The first major indication of the seriousness of the Government of India and the state governments with respect to making India ODF was demonstrated when they jointly earmarked a massive $20 billion budget for the programme. A significant portion of these funds was earmarked to be spent on Information, Education and Communication (IEC), signalling that behaviour change was to be at the core of this Mission right from its inception.

A major contributor to the success of SBM has been the policy shift towards an outcome-oriented approach, as opposed to an output-oriented one – focusing on eradicating open defecation as opposed to just building toilets. What has perhaps not been fully appreciated is that the concept of ODF itself was an early policy outcome of SBM. Prior to 2014, there had been different rural sanitation programmes in the country, but the focus of these programmes was more on constructing toilets (physical output) rather than mobilizing villages through behaviour change to become ODF (community outcome). The latter focus ensured that the entire community owned the responsibility of making their village ODF and local accountability shifted from the building of individual toilets to the community's responsibility for using peer pressure to achieve the 'last mile' conversion of the village to becoming ODF.

From a cautious beginning in late 2014, the first significant milestone was achieved in late 2015, with the tiny state of Sikkim becoming ODF. Thereafter, the next four states to become ODF were Himachal Pradesh, Kerala, Haryana and Uttarakhand, by late 2016. Today, in June 2019, almost all the states and Union Territories in the country are ODF.

Degree of Difficulty: Marketing a Product Not Many Wanted

Implementing SBM, the world's largest behaviour change programme, in a five-year time frame has not been easy. Building infrastructure like roads, houses or power lines, while no doubt challenging, is relatively uncomplicated: it takes resources and requires engineering and management skills. But changing behaviour in tandem with implementing infrastructure (construction of toilets) is an uphill task, with a very high degree of difficulty. We sometimes used to compare the SBM challenge with attempting to paint the wings of a plane in flight. Why was it so difficult?

SBM was complex and incredibly challenging because there was no obvious demand for toilets. Marketing gurus tell us that you may have a good product, but you still need to promote it because there may be other similar products in the market which compete with yours. In the case of SBM, the major competition to adoption of toilets was the deeply ingrained and centuries-old habit of open defecation. Demand for a toilet had to be stimulated to wean people away from the habit of open defecation and therefore a behaviour change campaign had to be designed and implemented *at scale*. At the same time, a massive infrastructure programme to construct toilets – close to a 100 million in rural India – had to be rolled out. This in itself was an incredibly challenging task and, given the scale of the country's geographical and cultural diversity, a decentralized and flexible approach was adopted for the supply of toilets at the local level. In most parts of the country, the preferred toilet technology option was the 'invented in India' twin pit–leach pit model, a low-cost, highly effective and environmentally friendly toilet.

Stimulating Demand: Behaviour Change at Scale

Disruption Begins at Home

While getting hundreds of millions of people in rural India to adopt and use toilets was going to be no easy task, we realized that behaviour change, like charity, has to begin at home. We, at the Ministry of Drinking Water and Sanitation, had to first change our own behaviour from scepticism about the success of such a mammoth programme to belief that it could be done. My colleagues in the

Ministry, while fully enthusiastic about the goal, were somewhat hesitant to wholeheartedly commit and do whatever it took to achieve it. We had to create a mini-disruption in the staid, low-profile Ministry of Drinking Water and Sanitation, shake things up and make our own colleagues in Delhi believe that the goal of an ODF India was doable. This included doing things differently, working in 'mission-mode' instead of following the traditional, non-time-bound approach to work in government offices, flattening out the organizational hierarchy, bringing in young and fresh talent from outside to take on new functions, such as agile planning, PR, communications, social media and rapid feedback on progress to districts, and even creating a clean environment in the Ministry by renovating the toilets in the building.

In the Ministry, the 'new normal' office timings became early mornings till late evenings. *ODF Saturday* video conferences with district collectors across India, *Lunch and Learn* workshops with field functionaries, and frequent travel to states, districts and villages became the practice. Disruptions were frequently carried out including the entire senior management of the Ministry. Bollywood stars and even the Comptroller and Auditor General of India shocked observers and the press when they volunteered to empty toilet pits themselves, demonstrating how the twin-pit design worked to convert toilet waste into safe and usable compost (the farmers of UP like to call this 'sona khaad' – gold compost).

The PM-CM-DM-VM Framework

Since sanitation is constitutionally a state subject in India's federal structure, the Union Government could only broadly play the role of a provider of financial and technical assistance and that of coordinator, convenor and monitor. Implementation of SBM, however, had to be done by the states, districts, panchayats and villages. SBM put into practice the concept of cooperative, competitive federalism by invoking the well-known Prime Minister–Chief Minister–

District Magistrate construct, and added its own innovation to this formula: the grassroots-level Village Motivator! PM-CM-DM-VM thus became the effective implementation mechanism. It took the combined effort of the Central, state and district teams, however, to operationalize this approach.

My team at the Ministry and I travelled extensively to different states to actively engage with and motivate all levels of state government officials to put SBM in mission-mode in their own domains. I myself have travelled over 150 times to the field, visiting each state at least once. I would typically call on the Chief Minister, impress upon him or her the importance of the programme, always meet the Chief Secretaries and request them to put SBM on their top-three list of state priorities and then, perhaps most crucially, meet and motivate the young DMs. I always learned the most from these young officers who were constantly innovating and coming up with local solutions to make their districts ODF. Full kudos to these young, bright and energetic civil servants fully committed to development at the grassroots level.

We also held frequent national and regional workshops with DMs and chief executive officers (CEOs) of districts from across the country to get them to share experiences and learn from each other. Recognizing the work of DMs/CEOs by honouring them with national awards, including those presented by the Prime Minister himself, encouraged a healthy, competitive spirit among young field officers, all the way from the district level to the block development officer and the panchayat sachiv, in the race to become ODF.

Behaviour Change on the Ground

Along with the DM, the village motivator (VM), or swachhagrahi, trained in community approaches to sanitation, and played a critical role in behaviour change on the ground through inter-personal communication with the village community. Today, SBM has over 6,25,000 swachhagrahis, on an average of one per village. The swachhagrahi uses an array of context-specific tools and techniques, including social mapping and extensive discussion at both the community and individual household levels to convince people about the usefulness of building a toilet and then using it. In some cases, the health factor works, i.e. making parents, especially mothers, realize that defecating in the open meant that flies would carry the excreta back to the food chain at home and consequently spread disease. In others, warning the community about the contamination of groundwater through open defecation is a strong motivator. Disgust at the shameful habit of open defecation would also be evoked. In the end, after an intense face-to-face discussion with the community, the village would get 'triggered' into accepting the fact that open defecation was not good for their community and committing to become ODF in the shortest possible time.

Behaviour Change through Mass Media

Many myths and stigmas persisted in rural India, acting as steep barriers to behaviour change. These included misconceptions such as (i) having a toilet on the household premises is impure; (ii) only women need to use toilets and it is okay for men to go outside; and (iii) someone else needs to clean my toilet. Such widespread stigmas had the effect of constraining the demand for toilets and needed to be effectively tackled. Mass media played a big role in dispelling such myths and misconceptions. SBM ran several such campaigns, strongly supported by our brand ambassadors, including Amitabh Bachchan, Akshay Kumar and Anushka Sharma. The Darwaza Band (shut the door on open defecation) I and II campaigns became big hits and were used across the country on all media platforms in different languages. This campaign focused on the use of toilets, especially by men and also on sustaining the changed behaviour over time. Akshay Kumar's Bollywood hit *Toilet: Ek Prem Katha* debunked the myth that it is impure to have a toilet at home and also encouraged women to stand up for themselves by steadfastly demanding a toilet for themselves. The radio campaign, Shaucha Singh, gave us a mascot who debunked these myths in all languages of India. Overall, the media – social, print, radio and television – played a big role in popularizing SBM and encouraging people to build and use toilets.

But it was not only the PM-CM-DM-VM formula and mass media programmes which resulted in behaviour change at scale. People from all walks of life adopted the SBM as their own and triggered a mass movement, aptly named a 'jan andolan' by Prime Minister Modi. Scale had to be addressed with scale and Team SBM leveraged a huge number of behaviour change agents across the country to lead the campaign. These included 12 crore school students, over 10 lakh masons, many of whom are women, 625,000 swachhagrahis, 250,000 sarpanchs, 700 district magistrates, over 500 young professionals (Zila Swachh Bharat Preraks) in the districts and over 50 national brand ambassadors. Needless to say, our Communicator-in-Chief, the Prime Minister himself, never missed an opportunity to talk about the importance of SBM and, from a national platform, motivated and exhorted his fellow countrymen to join and lead the programme to make the country ODF and swachh.

Such was the true involvement of all sections of society in this behaviour change effort that a 2019 study by the Gates Foundation has found that a communication spend of approximately Rs 25,000 crore was mobilized by SBM from various stakeholders, which is ten times the Government's budgetary investment in behaviour change efforts, i.e. Rs 2,500 crore. The study further estimates that, on an average, every rural Indian has been reached by SBM-Grameen messages at least 3,000 times in the last five years.

In fact, multiple surveys including *India Today*'s 'Mood of the Nation Survey', in the run-up to the 2019 general elections, found that SBM has made one of the strongest impressions on the respondents among government schemes. With a high number of women endorsing the programme, the government's initiative to provide safe sanitation right to their households has received widespread appreciation.

Keeping the Buzz Alive

The SBM jan andolan involves all age groups and sections of society, and we ensured that this people's movement manifested itself at regular intervals of time through tailored mass campaigns and large events with the Prime Minister. Be it the gathering of 6,000 women sarpanchs in Gandhinagar who were honoured by the Prime Minister for their contribution to Swachh Bharat on 8 March 2017 (International Women's Day), the mass triggering of behaviour change in Bihar by 20,000 swachhagrahis from across the country in April 2018 to celebrate the 100th anniversary of Gandhiji's Champaran Satyagraha movement, or the gathering of over 50 sanitation ministers from around the world, along with the UN Secretary General, in India to learn from the success of the Swachh Bharat Mission during the Mahatma Gandhi International Sanitation Convention (MGISC) 2019, the Mission has managed to stay relevant and exciting.

The autumn of 2017 witnessed over 5 crore primary schoolchildren across the country participating in swachhata painting and essay-writing competitions, resulting in mass awareness about sanitation. There was also active involvement of para-military personnel across the nation who participated in the making of short swachhata-related videos. This was followed by the Swachh Bharat Summer Internship in the summer of 2018, where over 4 lakh students and rural youth enrolled to perform swachhata-related activities across the country, including helping to dig toilet pits, clean villages and the dissemination of sanitation-related messages. Other events included the mobilization of over 20 crore volunteers for clean-up activities during the 15 September–2 October 2018 Swachhata Hi Seva campaign and the Swachh Sundar Shauchalaya (clean and beautiful toilet) toilet painting and decoration campaign in January

2019. The single biggest swachhata event during the entire five-year SBM period had to be the January–March 2019 Kumbh Mela, which was attended by more than 20 crore people. With over 1.2 lakh well-maintained toilets, it was almost universally acknowledged that this was truly a Swachh Kumbh, the likes of which had never been seen before. All of these campaigns ensured that the buzz of SBM remained alive and kicking. There was never a dull moment!

Sustaining the Changed Behaviour

Having achieved almost full sanitation coverage in the country, our focus over the past several months has been, and continues to be, on working with states, districts and villages to sustain the changed behaviour of toilet usage and make it last. Continuous efforts are needed at all levels to sustain behaviour change and efforts in this direction include ensuring that there are (i) adequate institutional arrangements at the Central, state, district and village levels for sustaining the change; (ii) appropriate financial incentives; (iii) continuing the IEC campaign; and (iv) strengthening the capacity of states, especially at the district, gram panchayat and village levels. Further, to keep the interest of the village community in sanitation alive, a detailed programme called ODF Plus, focusing both on ODF sustainability as well as on solid and liquid waste management (SLWM), is under implementation.

The Impact of SBM

The positive outcomes and impact of SBM are already being felt. First and foremost, the dignity and security of women and girls – the uncomfortable issue raised by Prime Minister Modi during his inaugural Red Fort speech – has been addressed by providing them privacy through the availability of individual household toilets. Broader health, economic and environmental outcomes of SBM have also been established over this relatively short period. A World

Health Organization study in 2018 found that SBM will have saved over 3 lakh lives by October 2019, with over 1 lakh lives expected to be saved on an annual basis after that. A UNICEF study in 2017 found that 82 per cent people felt that their status and prestige have increased due to SBM, and 87 per cent women felt safer after getting a toilet at home.

The same study found that the economic benefits of sanitation were very tangible at the household level. Their study estimated that in an ODF village, each family saves up to Rs 50,000 annually on account of reduced medical costs, time which can be used more productively, and lives saved. The study also concluded that the economic benefits of sanitation per household outweigh the cumulative investment (government spend plus other modes of financing including household contribution) by 4.3 times over a ten-year period.

Highlighting other significant health benefits of sanitation, the Bill & Melinda Gates Foundation (BMGF) conducted a study in 2017 that showed significant improvements in diarrhoea prevalence, stunting and wasting among children, and in the BMI of women in ODF areas, as against comparable non-ODF areas. Further, an environmental impact study conducted by UNICEF in early 2019 has revealed that, in terms of faecal contamination, non-ODF villages were, on average, 11.25 times more likely to have their groundwater sources contaminated (12.7 times more from contaminants traceable to humans alone).

SBM's positive ripple effect has spread to the creation of jobs as well. Direct employment opportunities have been created for masons, labourers and in industries supplying sanitaryware. Likewise, indirect employment opportunities have sprung up in several associated sectors. One estimate is that the achievement of an ODF India and the construction of about 10 crore toilets in the last 5 years generated over 90 crore person-days of employment.[2] The Toilet Board

2 Construction of one rural toilet requires an average of two labourers and one mason working for three days.

Coalition estimates that the sanitation market in India by 2021 will be a US $62 billion industry.

A very welcome result of SBM has been the empowerment of women and girls. Women, at all levels, have played a key role in the success of the programme, and SBM provided a unique opportunity for them to take a leadership role in their communities. Women comprised roughly 30-40 per cent of the volunteers – swachhagrahis – who led the process of 'triggering' behaviour change at the village level. The process of triggering depended heavily on surveillance committees – nigrani samitis – which had many women members, to persuade villagers not to defecate in the open. Women's self-help groups, Mahila Samakhya groups, and other such bodies were also drawn into the campaign. In many states, elected women representatives in panchayati raj institutions also played an active role in implementing SBM. The Mission also created an opportunity for entrepreneurship. A World Bank study in 2018 on the leadership role of women in the SBM presented accounts from the ground on how women took on the job of masons, a traditionally male-dominated profession, and earned money from toilet construction.

Everybody's Business

As a consequence of SBM, the idea of swachhata is now ingrained in the minds of most Indians and has also spread across sectors. The Railways have now achieved 'ODF' status as well: all railway carriages now have bio-toilets instead of the erstwhile iteration which had the opening for excreta to drop on to the track. All government schools in India now have separate toilets for boys and girls and all primary and community health centres have toilets as well. A Swachh Iconic Places initiative has also been implemented where some of the most important and iconic monuments of cultural, religious and tourist importance in the country have been made swachh to international standards. In addition, every Ministry celebrates a Swachhata Pakhwada in turn throughout the year, where sanitation-related activities are mainstreamed into their core programme. Further, each Department and Ministry now has a Swachhata Action Plan (SAP) which has a unique budget code (96), and is funded through the Department's own resources. The total funds committed for the SAP during the two-year period of 2017–18 to 2018–19 were over Rs 35,000 crore or about US $6 billion. Sanitation has now truly become *everyone's business*.

SBM's iconic logo of Gandhiji's glasses has become the nation's pride and a true symbol of the 'yes we can' spirit of our people and all that we can achieve together. In fact, one can find the SBM logo on currency notes, calling attention to the country's commitment to the cause. There is still much work to be done in the coming years, starting with the need to sustain our ODF status and also in implementing solid and liquid waste management, especially in urban and peri-urban India. But the good news is that sanitation has now firmly set its roots in the country's developmental agenda.

Key Lessons Learned – the 4 Ps

After almost five years of implementation experience under SBM, the key lessons we have learned could be categorized under four buckets, which were shared with the international community, including the UN Secretary General, at the MGISC in October 2018. These are the 4 Ps: (i) Political Leadership (ii) Public Financing (iii) Partnerships and (iv) People's Participation. This book is structured around the framework of the 4 Ps. The last P – People's Participation – was perhaps the most integral to the success of SBM. The programme ultimately succeeded because the people of the country adopted the programme as their own and made it a jan andolan, a people's movement, in much the same way as the Freedom Movement prior to 1947, when a mass people's campaign, led by Mahatma Gandhi, ended the British Raj. Led personally by Prime Minister Modi, SBM became another great people's movement, this time against open defecation, with similar spectacular results, ending with freeing India from open defecation.

Why This Book?

This book was conceptualized as a collaborative effort stemming from the very essence of sanitation being *everyone's business*. An incredible achievement like making India ODF could only happen with the coming together of a range of stakeholders through a range of partnerships. Its vision is to share the journey and implementation model of the programme which overcame the significant challenges of *scale, speed, stigma,* and ensuring *sustainability*. The book also attempts to capture the intricacies, complexities and scale of SBM and give the reader a sense of how it all happened from multiple perspectives. Each author brings an individual level of expertise in the sector, as well as a glimpse of having worked with the Mission in some capacity. Many of them are leaders in their respective fields and key contributors to India's development and growth story. From the lens of these authors, this compendium of essays attempts to provide a macro as well as micro perspective to cover the journey of SBM across topics. The essays in this book, categorized under the framework of the 4 Ps, provide a timely and crucial input to the national and global sustainable development agenda, and I am grateful to be able to share them with you.

My twenty-five years' experience in the water and sanitation sector has appropriately culminated in the pursuit of what many people thought was an impossible dream. The Swachh Bharat Mission turned out to be possible due to the vision and transformational leadership of Prime Minister Modi, which in turn triggered the jan andolan, perhaps the biggest behaviour change movement ever. I would like to sincerely thank each of the authors who contributed to this book. I hope that the readers enjoy the incredible story of the Swachh Bharat Mission through their essays.

POLITICAL LEADERSHIP

On 15 August 2014, in his first Independence Day address, Prime Minister Narendra Modi brought sanitation to the forefront of the national agenda. This established sanitation and cleanliness as a key developmental priority for the country in the years that followed.

Sanitation: A State Subject

RAGHUBAR DAS

Chief Minister of Jharkhand

IN JANUARY–FEBRUARY 2018, over 15 lakh rural women in Jharkhand got together and constructed nearly 3.5 lakh toilets during a month-long women's campaign called the Swachhata Sankalp Abhiyaan. Similarly, in June 2018, over 1 lakh rural households constructed toilets within just 11 days in Jharkhand as part of a mass people's campaign called the Swachhata Sahyog Abhiyaan. Later in the year, in November 2018, Jharkhand was declared Open Defecation Free (ODF). To put this in perspective, in 2014, Jharkhand had a sanitation coverage of less than 20 per cent, among the lowest in the country; less than one in five rural households in the state had access to a toilet.

This is the story of how Jharkhand went from being laggard to a leader in India's sanitation revolution.

Sanitation in the country had not been enough of a priority for any political dispensation at the state or Central levels for most of the seven decades since Independence. All this changed with the historic Independence Day address on 15 August 2014 from the ramparts of the Red Fort, when Prime Minister Narendra Modi challenged the country to eradicate the practice of open defecation in just five years, and take India from being the world leader in open defecation to the world leader in safe sanitation.

When I took charge as the Chief Minister of Jharkhand in December 2014, over 80 per cent of the population in the state lacked access to safe sanitation facilities. Given the effect that poor sanitation has on human progress and development, the fact that almost no one in India's political circles had spoken about it until Shri Modi took it up was shocking to me personally. I was fully aware of the chronic malnutrition, morbidity and stunting that open defecation caused among the children in India. Repeated bouts of preventable illnesses due to rampant pollution of our ground- and surface-water resources resulted in significant loss in the economic productivity of our workforce. Matters were especially difficult for women and girls who had to face the indignity and physical agony of waiting till dark to relieve themselves in the open. Many young girls chose to drop out of school once they reached puberty because of inadequate toilet facilities in schools, in essence depriving the state of scores of future women leaders.

With the Prime Minister putting his personal political capital behind this critical but until then unmentionable subject – a toilet – it gave me the strength and conviction to put sanitation on top of our state's developmental agenda. It was clear to me that the task of taking Jharkhand from among the states with the lowest sanitation coverage to an ODF state would have to be led personally by me, just like it was being led by the Prime Minister at the national level. As the Chief Minister, I could anchor the administrative machinery to focus on this by investing a significant amount of my time in the programme. This sent a strong signal down the line to all officials, especially district collectors, that sanitation was the top agenda of my government and it must be pursued relentlessly.

We had a long distance to cover, not only in terms of getting toilets constructed in all households, but also in convincing 2 crore rural people to shun their age-old beliefs and habits and adopt safe sanitation facilities. Changing the behaviour of people across 24 districts and 30,000 villages needed a well-articulated, well-thought-out strategy. We had to specially mobilize our women and involve those for whom the prevalent sanitation situation created a unique set of problems.

The Swachh Bharat Mission (SBM) recognized that the presence of a toilet in one's home is a necessary but not sufficient condition to end the practice of open defecation. In addition to infrastructural barriers, there are huge cultural and behavioural barriers that must be dealt with. Hence, the Government of Jharkhand adopted a demand-driven and community-centred approach that focused on both 'access' and 'use' issues, with an emphasis on information, education and communication. The programme had to be Government-facilitated, but at the same time it was people-led – a jan andolan – where everyone was motivated to collectively act on improving the sanitation situation in their villages.

To us, swachhata was not just about toilets; it was a catalyst for the larger goal of being a healthy state. We had Swachh Officials in each district and village to ensure that the people with access to toilets were using them and keeping them clean and hygienic. We created a cadre of swachhagrahis in each village who worked with the community to ensure that the village adopted sanitation practices, hygienic behaviours, and did not relapse to old habits. We also involved jal sahiyas – our women leaders in each village – to mobilize all women and men to agree on timelines and strategy to make their villages ODF. Our swachhagrahis and jal sahiyas played a key role in fast-tracking the sanitation movement in the state. The state Mission ensured that these jal sahiyas and swachhagrahis are adequately trained and financed to steer the sanitation drive in their villages. We learnt early on that the sanitation movement is best steered by local leaders and the state and district missions started recognizing and rewarding their efforts. This created further momentum and we could see common people providing exemplary leadership to the sanitation movement in the state.

We chose to promote the twin-pit toilet technology as it is most suited to the hydro-geology of Jharkhand, and people can easily use and maintain it. There were many districts within the state that had an acute shortage of masons. We needed trained masons in large numbers to construct the twin-pit toilets. But in this challenge lay an opportunity which eventually became one of the greatest social innovations of the Mission, probably in the entire country. In line with our philosophy of empowering women to take the leadership role in promoting sanitation, we started training the women of our villages as masons, and they came to be known as 'Rani Mistris' or 'Queen Masons'. Over 70,000 rani mistris were trained in the construction of twin-pit toilets as well as in behaviour change techniques within a year. This completely changed the supply-side landscape of SBM, and served as an inspiration to other women across the state to come out and voice their desire for a toilet in their homes. The rani mistris worked with the women of other households to build their toilets, spending 3-5 days with the family where the toilet was being constructed. They used this time effectively to trigger behaviour change and to impart all the information related to the maintenance of the toilet. As a result, all rural households in Jharkhand are now adequately informed not only of the technical design of their toilets, but also of the key hygienic practices that they must follow to realize the full benefits of improved sanitation.

Along with training rani mistris, several other initiatives were put in place to provide impetus to the ODF journey in Jharkhand. We trained 38,000 women swachhagrahis who undertook the task of educating people on the importance of sanitation and hygiene, along with its social, health and economic benefits. In Jharkhand, Swachhata Diwas is organized on the 19th of every month across all schools, anganwadi centres and health centres to further spread awareness and keep the buzz of swachhata alive in districts.

On the 2nd of every month, a Swachhata Sabha is organized across all gram panchayats where discussions on toilet usage and sustenance of ODF status are held so that the recently changed behaviours can be reinforced. Local nigrani samitis wake up early in the morning and go to the erstwhile popular open defecation sites to ensure that there is no slippage into old habits. I believe that the continuous involvement of local communities, especially the women's self-help groups, at every step of the sanitation ecosystem is one of the primary reasons for Jharkhand's success in eradicating open defecation.

I had announced that rural Jharkhand would become an ODF state in 2018 – a year ahead of the schedule announced by the Prime Minister to make India ODF. We have delivered on that promise. On 15 November 2018, at the state's Foundation Day event I had the privilege to declare Jharkhand free from the practice of open defecation. That Jharkhand has achieved the ODF status almost a year ahead of the national target is a matter of pride for all of us Jharkhandis.

We were able to achieve this because, right from the very beginning, our strategy has been demand-centric and our approach has been to make people understand the importance of toilets. Our behaviour-change campaign reached all and appealed to all segments of rural society uniformly. And most importantly, our efforts were accepted and amplified by the people of the state, so much so that several households opted to self-fund and self-construct their toilets, and surrendered the incentive that the Central and state governments provide for toilet construction. This illustrates the level of commitment that the people of the state have towards the process.

While we are proud of what we have achieved, we are equally conscious that there is still work to be done. We have already launched an ODF-sustainability guide for districts to follow and ensure that they remain ODF, and we are now taking this campaign beyond attaining and sustaining ODF status, to achieving an ODF-plus Jharkhand where safe sanitation will encompass complete solid and liquid waste management as well as plastic management. Waste water from kitchens and bathrooms will be treated and reused for agriculture and to recharge the groundwater. All villages will be equipped with rainwater harvesting structures to ensure availability of water for sanitation. Organic waste will be composted and converted into manure.

This process has already begun. Households are presently being trained to use cattle dung, household and agricultural waste extensively to produce biogas. This will not only ensure that villages in the state remain clean, but also strengthen the energy security of these villages.

The success of SBM is directly attributable to the political leadership provided to the movement by the Prime Minister of India. Shri Modi's leadership is manifested in establishing clear institutional responsibility and allocating budget for sanitation, and ensuring that all Ministries and Departments work together to make the country Open Defecation Free. He used his personal political capital to rally the citizens behind a common cause and set new priorities for the development agenda. He laid down a tremendous example for me to follow, and which I tried to follow to the best of my abilities.

With the guidance of our inspirational Prime Minister and the enthusiasm of the people of the state, I am confident that Jharkhand will continue to lead the sanitation movement and be a forerunner in the ODF-plus campaign as well.

Global Political Sanitation Alliances

KEVIN RUDD

Former Prime Minister of Australia

IF WE ARE concerned about lifting the world's population out of poverty, we cannot do so without addressing the world's problem of having safe drinking water and sanitation for all. It is the fundamental precondition. Others are important. This is *essential.*

I travelled to the Mahatma Gandhi International Sanitation Conference in New Delhi in September 2018 for a number of reasons. The first is that I am a great admirer of the Mahatma. We know him as the father of India's independence. We know him as the architect of non-violent political resistance around the world. But it was his passion for sanitation and cleanliness and hygiene in India's rural villages that truly sets him apart. Gandhi said, 'Sanitation is more important than political independence.' Imagine the strength in that statement, almost a century ago.

Gandhi also wrote, reflecting on his observations of the sacred river Ganges in 1919, 'I had gone there [to the Ganges] full of hope and reverence but while I realised the grandeur of holy Ganga and the holier Himalayas, I saw little to inspire me in what man was doing to this holy place.'

'To my great grief,' he said, 'I discovered in sanitation, both moral and physical ... There is defilement of the mighty stream even in the name of religion ... Thoughtless ignorant men and women use for natural functions the sacred banks of the river where they are supposed to sit in quiet contemplation and find God. They violate religion, science and the laws of sanitation.'

In May 1925, he wrote about the importance of keeping lavatories clean: 'The cause of many of our diseases is the condition of our lavatories and our bad habit of disposing of excreta anywhere and everywhere. I, therefore, believe in the absolute necessity of a clean place for answering the call of nature and clean articles for use at the time.'

In 1937, Gandhi received a letter asking what he thought was an *ideal* village and what problems he believed plagued the villages of India. Gandhi's response was: 'An ideal village will be so constructed as to lend itself to perfect sanitation ... The very first problem the village worker will solve is its sanitation.'

Gandhi's views on water sanitation were remarkable and visionary. He wrestled with great challenges in his time: getting rid of the British and cleaning up India. These were both noble causes in themselves, and he tackled them together. Mahatma Gandhi, for all of us, is seen as a great Indian nationalist. But he's also a great Indian internationalist – the whole world was part of his conscience.

Prime Minister Narendra Modi's Government has continued in Mahatma Gandhi's footsteps in pursuit of Sustainable Development Goal 6 (SDG 6). The Swachh Bharat Mission (SBM) was launched in 2014 from the Red Fort in Delhi as a statement to the people of India.

Since October 2014, 97 million toilets have been built in India (as of June 2019). Over 99 per cent of the population has access to a toilet compared to less than 40 per cent back in 2014. Over 622 districts in the country are classified as Open Defecation Free (ODF). Given the progress achieved thus far, it is estimated that SBM will have helped avert more than 300,000 deaths caused by diarrhoea, and protein energy malnutrition, between 2014 and when the programme draws to its conclusion in October of 2019 (WHO 2018). Unsafe sanitation caused an estimated 199 million cases of diarrhoea annually before the start of the Mission in 2014. These figures are now coming down.

None of this happens for free, of course. It comes at a cost. This is where the national political leadership comes in. It also requires the implementing bodies to deploy innovative sources of financing. Swachh Bharat has thus far required an investment of some US $20 billion. There's a message in that for all of us.

I write in my capacity as the Global High-level Chair of Sanitation and Water for All. This is an important partnership of over 200 governments, donors, civil society and private sector groups, research and learning institutions, and other development partners. We are a global family, and our partnership embraces the cause of sanitation and financing in countries around the world, and their aforementioned partners. If Mahatma Gandhi were alive today, he would see this as his mission.

Our aim is simple, but it is challenging: to turn SDG 6 into a reality. We can talk about it. We can think about it. We can have a lot of conferences at the United Nations about it. But unless we make it work, our people will continue to suffer. SDG 6 is about sanitation and water for all, to achieve which India's success is critical.

Many of our member states have seen great progress. For example, Ghana's Sanitation and Water Ministers recently launched a national sanitation and water programme to great acclaim. Their Mission statement was to 'Make Ghana the India of Africa'.

In Afghanistan, we now have developed separate budget lines for sanitation after the Afghan Finance Minister participated in our SWA High-level Meeting of finance ministers at the World Bank in 2017. The budget line helps them to clearly identify the resources necessary to turn universal sanitation into reality. They've also developed a Citizen's Charter that includes WASH as a priority. In fact, it is now a National Priority programme. We see the same in Burkina Faso, where the ministers responsible for water, sanitation and hygiene and finance jointly created a national platform to centralize WASH processes and provide innovative financing.

In Ethiopia, we see the 'One WASH' programme gathering momentum across the country. These countries are among many where progress is being achieved, taking inspiration from India's Swachh Bharat Mission.

How do you turn a vision into reality? Our vision is SDG 6. So what are the essential preconditions for making it work?

- National political leadership: As we've seen through the Modi Government's leadership, we need to bring about fundamental behavioural change in the people. It never used to be fashionable to talk about sanitation politically in our countries, but the national political leadership deems being able to talk about this effectively as a national political priority.
- Finance: It is estimated that bringing about the implementation of SDG 6 will require an annual additional global expenditure of US $114 billion per year. At present we are spending only US $35 billion each year in these key countries. There is a gap to be bridged through national budgetary allocations as well as innovative sources of finance from the social, community and private sectors. In projects of scale, this means attracting international finance as well. Finance must also be made sustainable so that these investments in sanitation can be kept up over time, instead of being abandoned due to lack of funds.
- Regular monitoring: We must also monitor our progress, to make sure that our vision, through national political leadership, financed by public or private or community sources, is being measured on the ground.

Central to the sanitation agenda is the importance of all the above for women. Unless we deal with this, we are failing our sisters across the world. Without access to clean drinking water, there are now nearly 300 million people, almost all women, carrying water to their families. This means young girls are not going to school. Or having gone to school, they have no opportunity to work because they're still burdened with this labour. Secondly, without access to safe sanitation at the household level, women are still compelled to defecate in the open, running the risk of being physically attacked or sexually assaulted. This is a problem across the world.

There is still another reason why sanitation is paramount for women: menstrual hygiene, a subject that in many cultures is often difficult to address. Unless we deal with the problem of providing adequate sanitation facilities for our sisters and for young girls across the world, this will remain a massive problem. A recent World Health Organization survey in India said that 43 per cent of Indian women did not have access to sanitary essentials at the beginning of periods. All of us, men included, need to become comfortable talking about these things in our politics.

There is nothing more fundamental for humankind than sanitation. The mission for us all has been laid out in the SDGs. We have the technology. We know how to bring about behavioural change. But the key element is finance – public, private or at the community level. All made possible through political will at the highest levels of political leadership. And in this, India stands out as an example for us all.

Swachhata and the Holy Ganges

UMA BHARTI

Former Union Minister for Drinking Water and Sanitation, Government of India

> *'Whoever throws dirt in the Street ... Whoever causes mire or water collection in the Street ... Whoever excretes faeces in pilgrim places, reservoirs, public places ... shall be punished with fines' and 'Nagaraka (City Superintendent) is punishable if he derelicts his duty' in the enforcement.*
>
> (Kautilya in *Arthashastra*, Chapter XXXVI, Book II)

FROM THE INDUS valley civilization to the vast Mauryan Empire, public sanitation was always given great importance in ancient India. As is so starkly pronounced by Kautilya, the ancient Indian states had punishment provisions for people polluting land and water.

Millennia since, through more than two centuries of colonization, India was driven to lose her connection with swachhata. That is, until 2014 – when the Prime Minister's clarion call to our mighty population of 130 crore people brought about a sanitation revolution never seen before by the world. The Swachh Bharat Mission (SBM) kept the focus strictly on behaviour change and created a community-based collective behaviour change movement, arguably the largest the world has ever seen.

Under the inspiring leadership of the Prime Minister, Shri Narendra Modi, who has been the torchbearer and chief communicator of the Mission, SBM has touched the right chord with every Indian. In the last five years, swachhata's enlightening message has reached all villages in rural India, with the participation of crores of Indians, and especially over six lakh swachhagrahis, our able ground force. As a result, as of June 2019 almost every Indian household has access to a toilet – an unimaginable state of things even five years ago.

My faith in our holy river Ganga is well known. The Ganga, deeply revered by all Indians, is the longest river in India, running through five states – Uttarakhand, Uttar Pradesh, Bihar, Jharkhand and West Bengal. Every day, thousands of devotees take a dip in the holy river, hoping for salvation. However, for many decades, unabated discharge of industrial and human waste had contributed to the pollution of this holiest of rivers. As a result, it figures among the ten most polluted rivers of the world.

To make the river clean again and initiate its conservation and rejuvenation, the Namami Gange programme was launched in June 2014 under the leadership of Prime Minister Narendra Modi. As the then Minister for Water Resources, River Development and Ganga Rejuvenation, it was my honour to lead this programme. It was based on the following key pillars: creating sewerage treatment capacity, riverfront development, river surface cleaning, biodiversity conservation, afforestation, industrial and direct discharge monitoring, and generating public awareness around the Ganga.

The programme has seen great success: 28 riverfront development projects and 33 entry-level projects for construction, modernization and renovation of 182 ghats and 118 crematoria have been initiated, and many completed. River surface cleaning activities for the collection of floating solid waste from the surface of the ghats and the river, and its disposal are afoot and pushed into service at 11 locations.

Several biodiversity conservation projects are underway, such as Biodiversity Conservation and Ganga Rejuvenation, fish and fishery conservation in the Ganga, and the Ganges River Dolphin Conservation Education Programme. Forestry interventions for the Ganga through the Wildlife Institute of India, Central Inland Fisheries Research Institute and Centre for Environment Education have been initiated. Forestry interventions for Ganga have been executed as per the detailed project report prepared by Forest Research Institute, Dehradun, for a period of five years (2016–21) at a project cost of Rs 2,300 crore.

Real-time Effluent Monitoring Stations (EMSs) have been installed in 572 out of 760 Grossly Polluting Industries (GPIs). Until now, the discharge into the Ganga of more than 500 drains has been stopped in Uttarakhand, Uttar Pradesh, Jharkhand and Bihar, and 63 sewerage management projects are under implementation in these states.

When I took charge of the Ministry of Drinking Water and Sanitation (MDWS), we brainstormed on how the Swachh Bharat Mission (SBM) might complement the goals of Namami Gange and how it can contribute substantially towards the swachhata of the villages on the banks of the Ganga. We have worked closely with states through which the river passes to ensure that all 4,465 villages in 1,662 gram panchayats on the banks of the Ganga have become Open Defecation Free (ODF) under SBM. This feat was achieved on 12 August 2017. Befittingly, a grand sammelan of the sarpanchs from all the panchayats concerned was organized at Prayagraj on that day and all present took an oath to keep villages on the banks of the Ganga clean. This success in a very short time period has been primarily due to the extensive engagements of the Ministry with the state governments, capacity building of the district magistrates, regular field visits and rigorous monitoring and follow-up.

A self-sufficient technology of faecal sludge management suitable to rural India, the twin-pit toilet technology was encouraged in these villages. However, making these villages ODF was not limited to toilet construction. A bigger aspect of the programme was to create awareness among the communities for sustained use of toilets, to keep their villages clean, not to use plastic, and to not have any direct untreated effluent discharge into the river. The people took an oath to preserve the sanctity of the river and never to pollute it.

At the same event in Prayagraj on 12 August 2017, MDWS, in collaboration with the National Mission for Clean Ganga (NMCG), launched the Ganga Gram Project, to create model villages on the banks of the Ganga with end-to-end solid-liquid waste management, cleanliness and development. This project was developed to have an integrated approach for the holistic development of the villages on the banks of the Ganga.

Some of the key objectives of the Ganga Gram Project are:

- Management of drainage system to stop waste water discharge into the river
- Groundwater recharge, conservation of local wells, ponds etc., conservation of groundwater and promotion of groundwater recharge
- Use of crematoriums with modern technology
- Complete management of village waste
- Coordination among various Government schemes on village development
- Promotion of medicinal plants, herbal plants and organic farming
- Tree plantation drives

A voluntary forum, the Ganga Swachhata Manch was formed to encourage local villagers, opinion makers, youth leaders and academic institutions to make these riverbank villages clean through a people's movement.

In order to strengthen the Ganga Gram Project and to make this movement a jan andolan, a series of activities such as public events, workshops, seminars and conferences and numerous Information, Education and Communication (IEC) activities have been organized to make a strong pitch for public outreach and community participation in the programme. Various awareness activities through rallies, campaigns, exhibitions, shramdaan, cleanliness drives, competitions, tree plantation drives and development and distribution of resource materials were organized and widely publicized.

MDWS has also been organizing Ganga Swachhata Chaupals in many riverbank villages. Recently, huge Ganga Gram Swachhata Sammelans were organized at five places: Sahibganj in Jharkhand, Buxar in Bihar, Kannauj and Bithoor in Uttar Pradesh and Srinagar in Uttarakhand in which thousands of rural women and villagers participated. Their overwhelming support towards Ganga Grams makes me confident that very soon we will restore the past glory of the Ganga.

I have attended all these sammelans and have told the villagers about the degenerating effect of open defecation and improper waste disposal. I normally ask them to take an oath with me to sustain the behaviour change, adopt clean and healthy habits, promote organic farming and preserve the sanctity of mother Ganga. We sensitize villagers to construct soak pits/leach pits at the household level and waste stabilization ponds at the community level, for grey water management.

MDWS, in coordination with NMCG and the Government of Uttar Pradesh, has also started a tree plantation drive in all the villages on the bank of Ganga. As of May 2019, approximately 1 crore trees have been planted to rejuvenate River Ganga.

The toilet access in rural India has already reached 99.3 per cent as of June 2019, and we need to not only sustain it but also to focus on ODF-plus interventions thoroughly. The villages along the riverbank have taken a lead in this regard, and I am sure that their enthusiasm for holistic swachhata will soon spread to the rest of the country.

Sometimes You Need to Get Your Hands Dirty. Happily.

RAJIV MEHRISHI

Comptroller and Auditor General of India

THERE WAS A time, not too long ago, when human excreta was not exactly a popular topic of conversation. It seldom came up in social discussions among adults, and definitely not among the top brass of the Government. But I faced no predicament when an old friend, and now the Secretary, Ministry of Drinking Water and Sanitation, Param Iyer, invited me to accompany him to empty out a pit full of decomposed excreta: my response was an unhesitating 'YES!' The invitation led to an experience that I will cherish forever – the opportunity to observe Bharatmata being made 'Swachh' at close quarters. And when I say close, I mean really close!

Sanitation, and the building of an Open Defecation Free (ODF) nation, always had to be everybody's concern. Like me, most Indians dream of a clean India. Then, the idea of shovelling excreta which is so completely decomposed that it is popularly called 'sona-khaad' should make no Indian, who calls himself 'educated', hesitate. If they do not lead by example, they are not really educated – merely (and at best) literate. Recall Gandhiji cleaning his own and his Ashram's toilets: the one truly educated Indian.

Within weeks of my first conversation about it with Param, I found myself in the beautiful city of Pune on a balmy Wednesday evening, having dinner with him, as he passionately explained to me the workings of the twin-pit toilet, which the Swachh Bharat Mission (Grameen) has been propagating for most of rural India. He explained in graphic detail how the toilet is made of two leach pits, each approximately 1 metre wide and just as deep. Initially, waste from the toilet is directed into one of the pits. The waste water leaches away from the pit and it takes around five years of regular use by a family of five for the pit to fill up. Once a pit fills, the household can redirect the waste to the other pit. While the second pit starts filling, the solid waste in the first one begins decomposing and in about a year's time, it decomposes completely, and is converted into compost that can be used in the fields as a fertilizer rich in nutrients, proven to enhance crop yield. Hence the name 'sona-khaad'.

The idea behind us emptying a pit was to make the point that this compost is safe to handle, and to defy myths and social stigmas around handling 'faeces'. It was also to practically demonstrate that people can empty the compost from their toilet pits themselves. Hardly a subject of regular dinner-table conversation, but this was the one real 'business' dinner I have attended, because what ODF implies is more than just a clean and disease-free India; it is the task of protecting the dignity of all rural Indians, especially the women.

The next morning, we woke up at the crack of dawn and began our drive to Daund block of Pune district, 85 kilometres from Pune city. This was where we were to meet Deepak Govind Jadhav and his family, whose toilet we had come to clean.

As an urban dweller, regardless of how many times you may have visited one before, there really is nothing like the beauty of a clean, well-mapped village. This was the sight that welcomed us to Pandharewadi Gram, home to Mr Jadhav and family. I knew that Maharashtra had declared itself ODF recently, yet the sight of a toilet standing, colourful and proud, in the veranda of each and every household in the village filled me with indescribable pride.

Deepak and his family stood outside their house, welcoming us warmly to their village and humble home. I wondered what they must have felt then, seeing a bunch of the distant bureaucrats who had come all the way from Delhi – and that too to clean out their toilet! We approached the pit which, we were informed, had filled over a year back and was full of compost by now. The lid was opened and we got right down to business. I jumped in with a shovel in my hand. There were no surprises. Exactly as Param had said: there was no odour whatsoever, not even the slightest, and to take my considerable weight, the compost had to be as solid as the land around the pit. I immediately set aside my shovel and started taking out the compost with my bare hands – the shovel was really just slowing me down in the narrow pit. One by one, our entire motley group – senior officers of the Government of India, Additional Chief Secretaries from many states and officers of the Government of Maharashtra – entered Deepak's toilet pit and mined wealth from waste, 'sona-khaad'. A truly memorable morning!

Back at home in Delhi that evening, I couldn't help but think about the progress figures of the Swachh Bharat Mission that Param had reeled off and given to me as part of my written brief. As of June 2019, these numbers stand at 9.7 crore toilets built in four and a half years, 30 states/UTs, 622 districts, 5.6 lakh villages declared ODF! Obviously, a mammoth achievement that should do us all proud.

The knowledge that Deepak's wife, the other women in his joint family, and their children, especially the girl-children, as well as *all* the households in that village were now using toilets, and were no longer shamed in the open, filled me with a mixture of deep satisfaction, pride, and lots of hope. We can indeed make India ODF, and restore to our fellow Indians the dignity they deserve. We can clean our cities, our villages, and our rivers. We can make India pure and 'Swachh'.

Role of the Federal

ARUN BAROKA

Additional Secretary, Department of Drinking Water and Sanitation, Ministry of Jal Shakti, Government of India

INDIA'S STRUGGLE FOR safe sanitation spans decades, with far-from-satisfactory results to show for it. Until 2014, that is. As reflected in the negligible fund allocation towards this cause, rural sanitation did not feature anywhere on the investment horizon in the first five plan periods. It did receive prominence from the Sixth Plan (1980–85) onwards amidst the launch of the International Drinking Water Supply and Sanitation Decade in 1980. In addition, responsibility for rural sanitation at the Central level was also shifted from the Central Public Health and Environmental Engineering Organization to the Rural Development Department.

In 1986, the Rural Development Department initiated the Central Rural Sanitation Programme (CRSP), India's first such programme on rural sanitation. The CRSP interpreted sanitation simply as the construction of household toilets, and focused on promoting the pour-flush toilets through hardware subsidies. However, the key issue of behaviour change to end open defecation and promote the use of toilets was not addressed adequately. As a result of this supply-driven approach the programme's impact in improving rural sanitation coverage was limited. Although more than Rs 660 crore was invested and over 90 lakh latrines constructed, rural sanitation grew at just 1 per cent annually throughout the 1990s. The Census of 2001 found that only 22 per cent of rural households had access to toilets compared to a rural sanitation coverage of 1 per cent in 1981.

In light of CRSP's limited impact on improving rural sanitation coverage, the Government of India restructured the programme, and launched the Total Sanitation Campaign (TSC) in 1999 and then the Nirmal Bharat Abhiyan in 2008. However, in the absence of strong political will and the requisite capacity needed at different levels to implement behaviour change, both these campaigns could not achieve the desired results.

Year 2014 – A Watershed Moment for Sanitation

15 August 2014 will go down in history as a watershed moment for sanitation in India, and arguably the world. In his first major address to the nation on India's Independence Day, sanitation was brought into the national consciousness by the Prime Minister of India himself, establishing its importance in his vision for India. During the launch of the Swachh Bharat Mission (SBM) on 2 October 2014, he urged each and every one to pledge that:

> *I will remain committed towards cleanliness and devote time for this. I will devote 100 hours per year, that is two hours per week, to voluntarily work for cleanliness. I will neither litter nor let others litter. I will initiate the quest for cleanliness with myself, my family, my locality, my village and my work place.*

Many 'experts' branded this as 'just another Government programme'. But to the people of India, it was evidently a lot more. The announcement touched the heart of the common man, and today rural India is poised to become open defecation free by 2 October 2019. What seemed like a dream in 2014 is turning out to be reality today.

Making of the Swachh Bharat Mission

SBM was designed using the learnings from the implementation of various sanitation programmes and aligned to the aspirations of people to collectively work towards achieving an Open Defecation Free (ODF) India. The task for us at the Ministry of Drinking Water and Sanitation (MDWS) was to first develop the strategic framework for the programme and, accordingly, the Ministry developed the SBM-Grameen (SBM-G) guidelines in consultation with various stakeholders. We adopted a Community Approach to Sanitation, putting people at the centre of the programme. The guidelines provided flexibility to states and allowed the people to plan, implement and manage the programme as suited to their needs and conditions.

The guidelines state that a village can be declared ODF by the community itself, at a gram sabha, once it has ensured that all households have access to a toilet and no one in the village defecates in the open. Provisions were also made for concurrent verification of the ODF status by the states. Every village declared ODF had to be verified within 90 days for its ODF status using a defined set of criteria by an external team from the district, and had to be re-verified 180 days from the first verification to reconfirm the sustainability of the ODF status. Nearly 90 per cent of the ODF-declared villages have already been verified using the ODF verification protocol developed by the Ministry.

Separately, the Ministry also commissioned the National Annual Rural Sanitation Survey (NARSS) 2017–18 and 2018–19, under the World Bank support project to SBM-G, using an Independent Verification Agency that surveyed randomly selected villages across states to assess the status of access to toilets, usage of toilets, solid and liquid waste management and ODF status of villages. States were incentivized based on their performance on the NARSS, and it became a very credible instrument to verify claims of states on key sanitation parameters.

Realizing that SBM would primarily focus on behaviour change, the guidelines allowed states to appoint professional staff at the state, district and block levels as well as in gram panchayats. This allowed states to augment their institutional capacities at each level and came very handy in implementing a behaviour change programme at scale. The states created a cadre of over 6 lakh volunteers – swachhagrahis – who worked with communities to achieve ODF status by focusing on sustained Inter-Personal Communication.

A rigorous Integrated Management Information System was developed to track the programme's progress, and monitor the sanitation access of each of the 17 crore households in rural India. Over 87 per cent of the toilets constructed under SBM-G have also been geotagged – an incredible feat in transparency.

A unique set of multipliers were brought together, catalysing progress for sanitation in their respective sectors. Inspired by the Prime Minister's firm commitment to SBM, the state and Central governments provided sufficient funds for this ambitious programme with a tight timeline. The world's largest government rural sanitation budget – to the tune of about INR 1,00,000 crore – was sanctioned and allocated as financial incentives to socially and economically weaker sections to construct and use toilets (@INR 12,000 per eligible household).

Business Unusual

The onerous task of providing all households access to sanitation in a given time frame called for out-of-the-box thinking and making courageous decisions. It also required working with various stakeholders and aligning them with the Mission's objectives. A national consensus and urgency had to be built to ensure that actors at all levels understood the approach, implementation design, and monitoring and measurement arrangements of the Mission. This called for partnerships, collaboration and conjoint action at all levels. We were treading a path never travelled.

Our motto was 'one vision one team' as we began by engaging all related Ministries at the national level. All Ministries developed their own Swachhata Action Plan to support SBM. At the state level we started building connects with Chief Ministers to lead the programme in their states. We met nearly all the Chief Ministers personally and this helped us unify our approaches, resources and actions to achieve results at scale and speed. Chief Ministers became effective communicators and champions of the Mission. Numerous meetings were held with Chief Secretaries of states, Principal Secretaries of departments managing SBM and Mission Directors to set timelines, dedicate resources and agree on the implementation strategy. The engagement with states has been unparalleled in the recent past and this increased engagement of the Centre with states has helped in fast-tracking the programme, collective reflection and renewed action.

We realized that the district collectors' leadership was key to ensuring speedy and effective implementation of the programme at the local level. We initiated a very informed and intensive engagement with district collectors along with the state governments to equip them with the needed technical and managerial resources to lead the programme. Workshops for district collectors, video conferences, learning lunches, etc. were organized at the Centre and in all states to build capacities.

A management dashboard was developed especially for the use of district collectors which allowed them to monitor the progress of SBM in every village in their districts on all critical parameters. ODF war rooms were established to coordinate, implement and monitor the programme in real time. Many collectors also conducted weekly review meetings with different stakeholders. These initiatives helped them identify gaps and fix issues on a regular basis.

And lastly, the sarpanchs, ably supported by the swachhagrahis, championed the cause of a Swachh Bharat at the cutting edge – the gram panchayat level. They provided local leadership, direction and inspired their communities to come together and make the Mission a jan andolan.

The sense of urgency percolated throughout the entire administrative system and ensured that sanitation remained everyone's top priority, and everyone's business.

Knowledge Management

A number of states undertook pioneering bold new initiatives to tackle the menace of open defecation, and made great strides towards collective and inclusive sanitation outcomes. The lessons emerging out of implementation at scale had to be effectively utilized through knowledge exchange platforms and workshops where stakeholders could share and learn from each other. Tailor-made technical support was designed to address challenges that arise during programme implementation. Knowledge was customized and distributed through a variety of channels: at learning events; by creating multi-stakeholder collaborative platforms; building coalitions; training; and facilitating knowledge exchanges. Joint annual reviews with states and districts were undertaken to assess progress, identify and propose measures to address any weaknesses, and identify and propose modalities for scaling up successes. A dedicated portal, Swachh Sangraha, was set up which helped stakeholders seek information on different aspects of programme implementation.

Regular video conferences (VCs) and workshops were conducted at the national and regional levels to get feedback from the field and promote the sharing of ideas. The VCs and workshops also helped the field-level functionaries understand the nuances of implementing such a scheme where behaviour change was the key. Champion collectors were duly honoured.

All these initiatives yielded significant increase in momentum on the ground. Further, regular calls were made to several stakeholders and updates shared on WhatsApp groups at all levels. Constant feedback from the field helped the programme immensely. Roll-out plans were meticulously formulated and critical input was welcomed at all levels.

Evolving Role of the Central Government

With SBM, the role of the Central Government changed drastically. MDWS no longer functioned like a typical Ministry, but like a Mission headquarter. Instead of allowing the Mission to proceed at its own pace, time-bound targets were agreed upon with states and requisite support was provided to achieve them. The Ministry assumed the role of co-financer, facilitator, collaborator and became an equal partner in achieving the Mission's objectives. It also shouldered the responsibility to create a unified vision, build a sense of urgency, as well as provide techno-managerial support to states and districts to achieve results at scale and speed.

With the final lap in sight, MDWS continues its efforts to not only achieve a Swachh Bharat, but also sustain it and deliver efficient solid and liquid waste management techniques. What had seemed unthinkable in 2014 is looking achievable in 2019, and India, in the Swachh Bharat Mission, has created a rare revolution that could improve the quality of life for its 130 crore citizens and lay the foundation for a truly prosperous future – one that will positively impact the country and its people for generations to come.

A Disruption Called Swachh Bharat

VALERIE CURTIS

Professor, London School of Hygiene and Tropical Medicine

THE CONVERSATION ABOUT 'shit' has been an uncomfortable one for many for decades, if not centuries. Any talk of faeces, or even toilets, has never been considered 'civilized' conversation. However, in 2015, when the Sustainable Development Goals (SDGs) were defined, open defecation and its health impacts were identified as one of the biggest challenges facing human health. 'Sanitation for all' is SDG 6.2 and the lion's share of the achievement of this goal relied on India, where nearly 60 per cent of the world's open defecators resided.

On 15 August 2014, as the people of India listened to their newly elected Prime Minister, Narendra Modi, deliver his maiden Independence Day address from the Red Fort, something remarkable happened. For the first time ever a Prime Minister of India addressed the nation on the subject of toilets. Why, he asked, was the shameful practice of open defecation rampant in the India of the twenty-first century? In his speech, he set the audacious goal of fulfilling Mahatma Gandhi's vision of a clean India by 2 October 2019, Gandhi's 150th birthday. It was a moment of disruption.

Behavioural science tells us that disruption requires three things: Surprise, Revaluation and Performance. *Surprise* because you have to get people's attention and tell them something new. *Revaluation* because you have to make people want change; show them a new world where things can be better. *Performance* because you have to make new behaviours possible in the settings in which they take place. This is as true of the behaviours of the masses as of the elite whose job it is to lead change.

Changing entrenched behaviour, like open defecation which has continued for centuries, isn't easy, however. In the Swachh Bharat Mission, I witnessed behaviour change which started at the top – the policymakers! The Prime Minister surprised everyone by placing the unexpected subject of open defecation right on top of his agenda in 2014. His team set out a vision of a clean India that made people revalue and desire toilets. The performance of the Government team was disrupted by doing many things differently from business-as-usual. So how did this happen?

Disrupting Behaviour Settings

Governments the world over have fixed patterns of behaviour and those habits are completely predictable. This is because an office is what is known as a 'behaviour setting', where established roles, routines, rules and objects dictate daily activity. The everyday routines of office work, for example, are pretty much the same – the 9 a.m. start, tea break, lunch break, and finally the 5 p.m. close of business. All officials know their role, their job, and how it fits in the hierarchy of other roles in the organization. The objects they use are the same everywhere. Piles of files lie on real or virtual desktops, waiting to be processed using real or virtual writing instruments. As a result, no one has to think much about what they are doing; behaviour runs on auto-pilot. Any deviation from the established pattern is met with disapproval, or some other form of sanction.

Political disruption succeeds only when it is translated into *disruptive action* by the administrators on the ground. Staff at the Swachh Bharat Mission-Grameen (SBM-G) sat down and started figuring out what they would have to do to meet this challenge. Working with states to change the age-old habits of 550 million people by building them 100 million toilets in only 1,825 days seemed an impossible task. One thing they knew: business-as-usual was not going to do the trick. They would have to start with disrupting long-standing habits in their own backyards.

Roles Were Disrupted by Bringing In Young Blood

The Swachh Bharat team at the Ministry of Drinking Water and Sanitation realized that if it was to achieve the seemingly impossible goal of an Open Defecation Free (ODF) India it had to become a disruptor; it had to change something in the behaviour settings of fellow Government officials throughout India.

So the team members set to work. First they redefined their own *roles*. Instead of functioning as simply Government workers, they started working in mission-mode, with one objective: to make India ODF by 2019. New roles were created by bringing in young blood to take on new functions, such as agile planning, communications, social media and rapid feedback on progress to districts. No longer did normal office *routines* apply. The SBM-G staff found themselves in the building at dawn, often leaving late at night. Lunch breaks became informal seminars on the topic of toilets. The office itself was discarded as a work setting with a large number of days spent on the road and in remote rural districts, to spur the people on. Rules were broken. For example, the Secretary shocked observers when he volunteered to empty toilet pits himself, showing how the twin-pit design worked to neutralize toilet waste.

On the ground, an army of swachhagrahis was recruited and trained to trigger behaviour change concerning toilets in thousands of villages. Instead of following the rule book, districts were encouraged to make up rules for themselves, spurring grassroots innovation, mass-mobilization events, and sharing inspiring individual stories of people who had made their villages ODF.

Did Disrupting Government Settings Work?

SINCE OCTOBER 2014, it is reported that over 97 million new households toilets have been constructed (as of June 2019), and millions of older toilets which had become dysfunctional have been retrofitted. Over 85 per cent of the new toilets have already been geo-tagged, and their pictures are available in the public domain. These efforts have taken the national rural sanitation coverage to over 93 per cent according to the National Annual Rural Sanitation Survey 2018–19 (under the World Bank support project to SBM-G).

As a result, more than 550 million people have changed their behaviour and stopped defecating in the open. The World Health Organization estimates that the Mission will have saved over 300,000 lives in the five years since its inception, if India can reach its stated goal of 100 per cent toilet coverage by October 2019.

It is only fitting that Swachh Bharat is celebrating its extraordinary success in this 150th birth year of Gandhi. The celebrations were kick-started with the Mahatma Gandhi International Sanitation Convention in New Delhi in the run-up to 2 October 2018 with Prime Minister Modi, the UN Secretary General and Ministers for sanitation from over fifty countries. The participants who attended learnt how disruption of business-as-usual has been key to the success of the Swachh Bharat story and that this has mobilized millions to care about, and act upon, this most unlikely of causes.

The Lesson in the Success of Swachh Bharat

The Swaach Bharat Mission shows that behaviour can be modified, both at the level of policy and in society. Now, from not being comfortable even talking about toilets, the discourse has changed to the extent that ornaments that look like 'shit' are now sold at gift shops! India would not have been able to transform its sanitation behaviour without surprising everyone by beginning a dialogue about toilets, making them culturally valued, and without making performance possible by disrupting the settings of everyday behaviour in Government offices and amongst millions in India.

Much of our daily behaviour is routine, standard, unchanging and unthinking, deeply embedded in the settings of everyday life. These fixed patterns can be hard to change. But if we want to make a difference, whether in our personal or in our professional lives, we need to find disruption points. We need to change the objects, routines, roles or rules that keep us on autopilot and tell us what to do. Only then can we achieve audacious, transformative goals for ourselves, and our nations.

A People's Pursuit of Sanitation: The Story of Jashpur District

PRIYANKA SHUKLA

Former District Collector of Jashpur

SHALIMA NISHAD, A student of class 7 from Jashpur district in Chhattisgarh, wrote an emotional 'appeal' to her parents on 30 April 2016 (the day when schools were closing for summer vacations), just like the other 69,663 schoolgoing children in the district. All she wanted was to get a toilet built for her family before the school re-opened. She was a tad more persuasive and persistent than some of her friends – who made a similar demand – which compelled her 'Daau' to build one for her in the first week of May itself. After all, Shalima wanted to be the best amongst all swachhata balveers of the district – a recognition which many of her age, living in big cities, would hardly think of striving for.

Constant motivation by Ms Ursela Toppo, a primary-school teacher in Kunkuri, Jashpur, led to the construction of toilets by twenty families. Similarly, Rohit Lakda, president of the college social group 'YUVA', along with his group members, started a campaign in early August 2016 where they reached out to the owners of the local eateries (dhabas and small hotels) of the district, asking them to build and use toilets. Courtesy of the effective 'triggering' led by these youngsters, four of the eateries completed the construction in twenty days.

When the women of village Geedha in Jashpur district, while fasting for their husbands' long life on Haritalika Teej, also observed a swachhata upawas, it became evident that the impetus for change is not merely a trickledown effect, but is spreading from the ground up. The women said they observed the fast so that their 'prayers to ensure that their district becomes Open Defecation Free are answered at the earliest'.

Quite evidently, a revolution of sorts took place in Jashpur. Such stories of incremental but substantive change abound in the district. This is a change that is palpable not just in outcome but in a transformed mindset. This outcome has not resulted from fear or force but from sheer willingness to be a part of the change. Jashpur is located in north-eastern Chhattisgarh – about 500 kilometres from the state's capital. Almost 67 per cent of the population belongs to tribal communities (including Particularly Vulnerable Tribal Groups like Pahadi Korwas and Birhors) and more than 40 per cent of its area is under forest cover. It is a very picturesque district, endowed with natural beauty and blessed with simple natives whose endearing smiles and warmth will win you over in just a second.

Just like the entire country, in Jashpur too, implementation of the Swachh Bharat Mission (SBM) started way back in 2014, with the Prime Minister making a historic clarion call to the nation for a Clean India by 2 October 2019, the 150th birth anniversary of Mahatma Gandhi. By 31 March 2016, however, of the 427 gram panchayats and 766 villages in Jashpur, only 21 and 43, respectively, had been declared Open Defecation Free (ODF). It was only in April 2016 that, to ensure that Swachh Bharat gathers greater momentum in the district and to ensure the sustainability of the changes thus brought about, the Jashpur district administration took initiatives to make the programme more people-centric. After all, to bring about a long-term change in the sanitation scenario, active participation of local people was much more important than mere construction of toilets.

From a Government Initiative to a People's Movement

From April 2016, a series of interactive sessions were convened by the district administration. All grassroots-level workers – 397 panchayat sachivs, 201 patwaris, 2,946 anganwadi workers, 406 ANMs (auxiliary nurse midwives), 3,573 mitanins etc. – were sensitized and trained to educate and motivate people. Workshops were convened with all 6,915 people's representatives of the district to make sure that each one of them understood the need and the importance of sanitation. The district administration machinery deputed 214 nodal officers to sensitize and trigger two gram panchayats each. In fact, till date, in every public meeting, sanitation-related behaviour change is the foremost discussion point for the entire district administration.

Natural Leaders from the Community: The Crucial Motivators in SBM

The identification of various natural leaders as Community Resource Persons (CRPs), their capacity building regarding Community Approach to Sanitation (CAS) techniques at regular intervals, district-level experience sharing workshops and motivational sessions for them at regular intervals were important aspects of the district's key strategy.

Many such CRPs were intelligent enough to search for village-specific trigger factors themselves. For example, natural leaders in Basantala village realized that open defecation exposed them to elephant attacks, which led to the death of many locals. They used it as trigger factors and explained to villagers that such mortalities could be effectively minimized by the construction and use of toilets. Within no time, the villagers understood the gravity of the message and started working towards making the village ODF. Felicitating such natural leaders was an integral part of the campaign to keep their motivation and enthusiasm intact.

Swachhata Balveers, Chauwa Tolis and Teelu ka Toilet: Changing Things the Children's Way

John F. Kennedy once said, 'Children are the world's most valuable resource and its best hope for the future.' School Led Total Sanitation (SLTS) was, thus, made the linchpin of the SBM campaign in Jashpur. Children not only understand things easily, they zealously disseminate them as well. Innovations like dedicated comic booklets for children, educating them about the need for toilets, were circulated in schools. They include *Sh se Shauchalay* and *Teelu ka Toilet*. (The success of *Teelu ka Toilet* later inspired Nellore district to have the book published in Telugu as well). Sanitation-related nursery rhymes and mathematical tables got the best response from children.

The formation of Chauwa Tolis (groups of children who undertake door-to-door visits in their village on Sundays and sing songs in the local dialect to motivate behaviour change) was yet another important success point. More than 2,000 Chauwa Tolis were formed in the district. All those children who thus succeeded in getting a toilet made were felicitated as Swachhata Balveers (142 as of now). The creation of the post of Swachhata Mantri in various schools and the construction of attractive school toilets (designed as Swachhata Express) to instil a liking for swachhata in schoolgoing children succeeded in ensuring that children become the most effective harbingers of social change on this front. Menstrual hygiene management was taken up as a special component of the campaign and thus Pyari Bitiya Camps are being organized in the district. About 15,000 adolescent girls participated in such awareness camps in the district.

Teacher-led Special Initiatives in Jashpur

Swachhata Corners were established in all schools of the district. Teachers of all 108 schools of Manora went one step ahead and got an innovative Swachhata Rack (for Rs 155) made all by themselves for their school students so that everything related to hygiene (comb, nail cutter, soap etc.) could be stacked neatly.

Special events were organized by teachers, e.g. celebration of ***Swachhata se Mitrata*** **Diwas** on Friendship Day 2016 by more than 6,000 members of shikshakarmi federations and farmer producer organizations in Jashpur. On this day, they not only took out rallies in various villages but also made visits to about 20,000 families, gifted them flowers and requested them to build and use toilets, thus befriending swachhata for a lifetime. Forty-two of them also gifted toilets to some of the financially backward women as a Rakhi gift.

Swachhata tables and Swachhata nursery rhymes were painted on walls of various schools by school teachers and also proved to be immensely popular amongst schoolchildren.

Quite Literally: Celebrating the Spirit of Swachhata by Including It in Local Festivities

> From Raksha Bandhan to Diwali, many festivals fall around this time of the year. Why don't we associate each festival with cleanliness? You will see, the tradition will become a habit.
>
> – Narendra Modi on 'Mann Ki Baat', 30 August 2015

In a country like India, which is known for its festivals, using these occasions to motivate people to embrace SBM came handy and added new vigour to the movement. To make the campaign more popular, for almost two years, almost every festival in Jashpur was linked with swachhata. The district celebrated Swachhata Bandhan Diwas one month before Raksha Bandhan, Independence Day as Hum Honge Kamyab – Swachhata se hi Swatantrata Day and Swachhata Ashtami on Janmashtami.

Innovation: The Key to Success

Music is a way of life in Jashpur, so it had to be made a part of the campaign which was to be led by people. Apart from the routine kala jatthas and the rural sangeet tolis, Jashpur has a unique distinction of having a swachhata music band of its own. The band, called Jashpur Jhankar, is one of its kind as majority of its members – like Shri Sandeep Sharma, its lead singer and a panchayat secretary – are grassroots-level Government functionaries. Courtesy of the band, Jashpur also has a swachhata anthem of its own in Chhattisgarhi which inspires people more than anything. Competitions like Raj Mistri Number 1 were organized to motivate the masons.

Giving the Campaign a Personal Touch

To give the Mission a personal touch, the district collector and chief executive officer of the zila panchayat rolled out initiatives like writing 11,500 letters to brothers and sisters of the district on Rakhi, requesting them to build and use toilets, thus actually fulfilling the promise of protection that brothers give to their sisters every year on this occasion. Public representatives, like the zila panchayat president, Mrs Gomati Sahu, wrote letters to 5,000 natives of various gram panchayats which had been declared ODF to ensure sustainability of the usage of toilets. Even doctors of the district regularly prescribed the construction and use of toilets to patients who did not have or did not use toilets.

Since it shares borders with different states, the local dialects in Jashpur change every 50 kilometres. For effective communication of the message, the swachhata pledge, songs, etc. were drafted in all dialects like Surgujiya, Chhattisgarhi, Oriya, Kudukh as well as Saadari.

Strategy and Action Plan

- Gram panchayat-level/cluster-level/block-level teams were formed for implementation and monitoring.
- Data collated through a baseline survey was taken as reference point for demand and goal assessment – provisions were also made for any new households which came up post the survey in any village.
- After the assessment of the goal, master trainers were deputed at the district level who would lead the behaviour change movement through CAS teams led by Swachhata Preraks. The number of masons required was calculated and accordingly sufficient number of masons were trained at the district, cluster and block levels.
- Adequate mechanisms were established to ensure regular reporting to the district control room every single day. Reports from gram panchayats and clusters were compiled at the block level and submitted to the district. WhatsApp groups were also made to make the reporting easier. Future interventions were planned on the basis of these day-to-day reports.
- A material chain was established to ensure that interruption of supplies did not impede the construction. Regular meetings of suppliers were also convened at the district and block levels. SHGs which made bricks, etc. were also made a part of the chain. Special mechanisms were devised for remote areas chiefly inhabited by PVTGs like Pahadi Korwas and Birhors.
- Women SHGs led the movement all through Jashpur.
- Powerful sanitation messages were widely publicized in the district through wall paintings and slogan writing on all major buildings in the gram panchayats. SBM-specific milestones

and pictorial messages were displayed on national highways, all major crossroads, etc.

- Various campaigns like Darwaza Band Rallies, Swachhata Bandhan Fest, Gratitude Fest, Swachhata Selfie contest, Swachhata Sangoshthis, etc. were organized from time to time to maintain the zeal and enthusiasm in the district team.
- Felicitation programmes were organized regularly to boost the morale of the ground team, especially of swachhata champions – women SHG members, field functionaries, public representatives, school/college students, teachers, etc. and those block-level/district-level officials who walked the extra mile to ensure that the entire district becomes ODF.
- Exposure programmes were also organized for Swachhata Preraks, women SHG members, public representatives, etc. to visit nearby gram panchayats, blocks and districts to promote peer learning.

The Way Forward

As Robert Frost famously said, 'The woods are lovely, dark and deep/But I have promises to keep/And miles to go before I sleep'. In the context of the sanitation scenario in Jashpur too, while the change in the mindset of the people and the resulting outcomes are visible and heartening, it is important to keep the momentum going. Ensuring provision of piped water in the remotest areas, ensuring long-term sustainability and toilet usage by all at all times, provisions for solid and liquid waste management in all gram panchayats together form the way forward. But then, for a team as committed as the Jashpur team, there is no challenge too big to meet. Be it the district administration, be it public representatives, be it natural leaders or be it the community itself – the entire Jashpur team is determined to tackle every obstacle in its path with zeal, enthusiasm and dedication to ensure that this change that we have achieved with a lot of hard work and determination is sustained for all time to come.

As the eminent Hindi poet Shri Harivansh Rai Bachchan, rightly puts it:

Lehron se darr ke nauka paar nahin hoti
Aur koshish karne walon ki kabhi haar nahin hoti.

Swachh Nigeria 2025

SULEIMAN H. ADAMU

Minister for Water Resources, Government of Nigeria

NIGERIA IS A nation of great people with an estimated population of 191 million as of 2018. Located in sub-Saharan Africa, it is a large country with tremendous natural and human resources. However, Nigeria faces a critical challenge in its Water, Sanitation and Hygiene (WASH) sector. While it has made significant progress in improving national access to better water supply from 40 per cent in 1990 to 69 per cent in 2015, there has been a great decline in access to piped water on premises from 32 per cent in 1990 to 7 per cent in 2015, in urban areas. The national access to basic sanitation stands at a meagre 33 per cent, with an estimated 47 million persons practising open defecation, the second highest globally.

During the Millennium Development Goals (MDGs) era, the country made several efforts towards improving access to sanitation. These included the adoption of the Community-Led Total Sanitation (CLTS) approach to scale up sanitation in rural areas. National and sub-national specific roadmaps were also developed towards the close of the MDGs era for the elimination of open defecation in the country by 2025. The operationalization of the roadmaps across the country was, however, slow and inconsistent. A new programme, Partnership for Expanded Water Supply, Sanitation and Hygiene

(PEWASH), was initiated in 2016 to improve the situation and bring sector actors together.

Nigeria and India share similarities, which include not only a large population, but also a decentralized government structure and challenges in the WASH sector. This has also unfortunately led to our countries occupying top positions on the global open defecation ladder. However, India's ongoing Swachh Bharat Mission (SBM) has led to an incredible reduction in the number of people practising open defecation in just five years, and the country is on its way to becoming Open Defecation Free (ODF) by 2019. This has greatly challenged Nigeria, as it is set to become the next global leader in practising open defecation once India meets her target.

Nigeria prides herself on a number of achievements and triumphs globally. But the trophy for open defecation is not one we are looking forward to having. The success of SBM is an inspiring model for Nigeria and plans were already being made for a Nigerian delegation to visit India when I received an invitation to the Mahatma Gandhi International Sanitation Convention (MGISC), scheduled to be held in September–October 2018.

My participation in the MGISC was truly inspiring. It afforded an opportunity to interact with delegates from across the world and provided a platform for me to share Nigeria's modest effort at financing rural sanitation. Most importantly, I was able to get the real feel of SBM and the dramatic change it has wrought in India's sanitation story within so short a time. I was awed and sold.

The Sustainable Development Goals (SDGs) for water and sanitation are quite ambitious compared to the MDGs. The cross-cutting nature of water and sanitation means that they directly and indirectly impact the achievement of the other SDGs. The huge population of India hitherto practising open defecation, which has been drastically reduced through the Swachh Bharat Mission, will contribute significantly to the attainment of SDG 6 globally.

Since becoming Nigeria's Minister for Water Resources in 2015, I had wanted an initiative that would create a mass movement, with every citizen effectively mobilized for action towards achieving SDGs 6.1 and 6.2 on water and sanitation. While our ODF roadmap indicated rolling out a campaign at the national and sub-national level, a clear-cut strategy for carrying this out was not in place. My Ministry, in collaboration with our development partners, has been in the process of developing this strategy. A special unit within the Ministry was created for this purpose.

From the MGISC, I have come to the realization that focusing on such a high priority programme in mission-mode will make the campaign more effective and efficient. The Nigeria ODF campaign is now being remodelled on the same lines as SBM.

Like India, Nigeria has been able to demonstrate a high-level political will for the WASH sector. In November 2018, President Muhammadu Buhari declared a state of emergency and launched a new National Action Plan for the sector. The plan has five components – governance, sustainability, sanitation, funding and financing, and monitoring and evaluation. It proposes an eighteen-month Emergency Phase, five-year Recovery Phase and thirteen-year Revitalization Strategy for the sector. It also proposes the establishment of a National WASH Fund to incentivize reform and infrastructure revitalization.

In February 2019, the federal governments of India and Nigeria collaborated, with the support of international development agencies, and organized a study tour to help Nigerian delegates gain insights into how the application of SBM can help achieve similar sanitation targets in the Nigerian context. The study mission, which lasted almost two weeks, presented learning opportunities that could be potentially fruitful to Nigeria's national roadmap for becoming an ODF country by 2025.

SBM stands to inspire other countries, as it has done mine, and is a testimony to the global community that SDGs are achievable, provided there is strong political resolve, the strategy is appropriate, resources are adequately deployed and the population is sufficiently mobilized.

Looking ahead, it is my hope that, following India's example, Nigeria will not only be able to end the practice of open defecation among her populace, but will also become the next shining example to countries in the African region and across the world. It is my hope that the bilateral relationship between Nigeria and India will be further strengthened as we eradicate open defecation together.

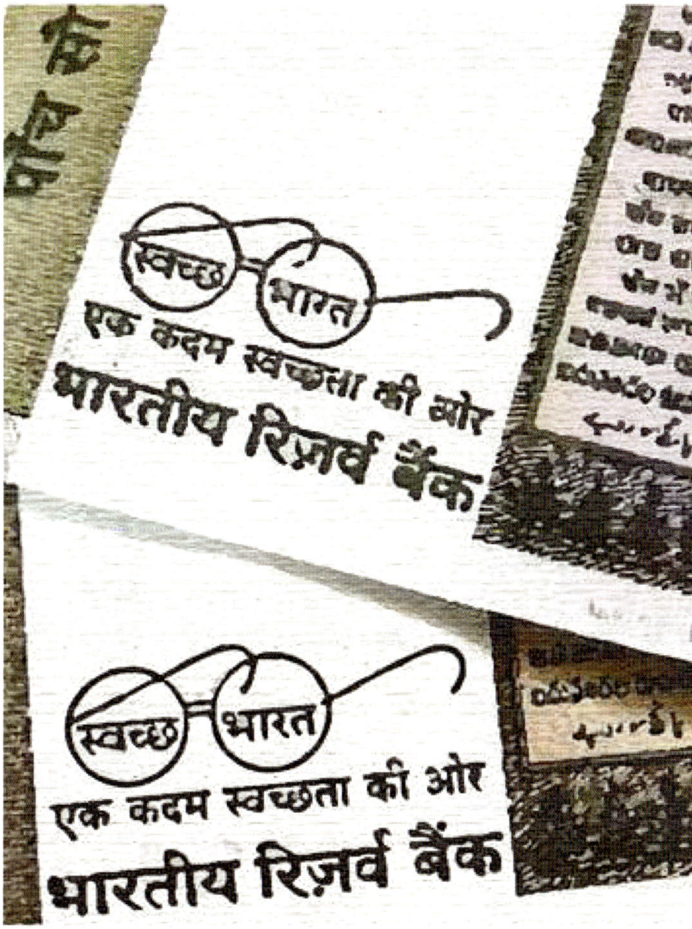

PUBLIC FINANCING

To ensure the success of the Swachh Bharat Mission, the Government of India allocated a cumulative budget in excess of \$20 billion from 2014 to 2019, one of the largest government sanitation budgets in the world.

Money Where the Mouth Is

ARUN JAITLEY

Former Union Minister for Finance, Government of India

WHEN JOHN F. Kennedy announced in 1961 that the United States would put a man on the moon by the end of the decade, no one thought it was possible. But it was accomplished in the next eight years. When Narendra Modi declared in 2014 that India would be Open Defecation Free (ODF) by 2019, changing the sanitation behaviour of close to 60 crore people who practised open defecation at the time, no one thought it was possible. Today, less than five years later, India is on the cusp of eradicating open defecation.

Sometimes a big, hard, audacious – and seemingly outlandish – goal set by a strong leader brings out the best in people and institutions. It takes them out of their comfort zone, makes them think big and aim high. It makes them push the boundaries of their imagination by painting a picture of what success will feel like. It motivates them to deliver beyond their pay grade, and punch above their weight, and the sum becomes greater than the parts.

Till 2014, what many of us take for granted – a toilet – was something millions of people in India could not even imagine having access to. Women, particularly in rural areas, wanted toilets, but could not voice their need openly and strongly, and often had to sacrifice it for a television set or a motorcycle. This was the elephant in the room that no one was really addressing seriously.

But as they say, no one can stop an idea whose time has come! No less than the Prime Minister of India issued a war cry against this indignity from the ramparts of the Red Fort in his first Independence Day address to the nation. He still talks about toilets unabashedly at various public gatherings. Suddenly, the 'unmentionable' toilet has been placed at the forefront of India's developmental and political discourse. The Swachh Bharat Mission (SBM) is discussed everywhere, from tea stalls and gram sabhas to panel discussions on national television. This acceptance of a toilet as an important aspect of everyday life that merits discussion, not just locally, but nationally, was a watershed moment in India's journey to successfully ending open defecation.

To make this ambitious goal a reality, we had to back it up with adequate resources. It could not have been an unfunded mandate. As the Finance Minister of the country, I had the unenviable task of allocating resources to various important Government programmes and sectors, all of which are equally important and deserving of investments. However, unlike previous administrations, for us the overarching importance of sanitation in the wider development of the country was fairly intuitive. As the fastest growing major economy in the world, India is committed to improving the quality of life of its citizens, especially in rural areas. We were already doing a lot of work on enhancing roads and providing electricity and housing, and access to sanitation, which in many ways is fundamental to human development, had to be front and centre of our development plank.

That said, what made my job easier was the understanding that good sanitation is good economics. Not only did poor sanitation undermine the safety and dignity of the women in our country, but it also caused our children to suffer repeated bouts of diarrhoea, which hindered their physical and cognitive development. This would adversely affect the productivity of our nation's future workforce and what is India's biggest economic competitive advantage – our demographic dividend. What's worse was that this had become a vicious cycle. Frequent illness hampers the learning abilities of children, leading to poorer schooling outcomes and the children grow up to have a skill set that is sub-par compared to their true potential. As adults, they are not able to provide better living conditions for their children, who in turn remain stunted or wasted. Stunted or wasted children are less likely to break out of abject poverty.

The World Bank had estimated that the lack of sanitation cost India over 6 per cent of its GDP every year. I believe the gains from investing in sanitation are much higher than any percentage of GDP could articulate. India backed this lofty goal with a handsome budget: over Rs 1.3 lakh crore (over $20 billion) in five years, shared between the Centre and states in a 60:40 ratio (90:10 for special category states). Over 8 crore marginalized households, including all scheduled castes, scheduled tribes, women-headed households, and small and landless farmers were offered a financial incentive of Rs 12,000 to construct a toilet in their homes. Significant allocations were also made in promoting behaviour change through Information, Education and Communication (IEC) activities at the mass media as well as at the inter-personal level. In fact, a recent study by the Bill & Melinda Gates Foundation pegged the leveraged monetary value of the IEC under SBM at over Rs 26,000 crore.

In addition to this large public funding towards improving sanitation, consistent efforts have also been made to leverage investments from the private sector, developmental agencies, faith-based institutions, and even citizens. The Swachh Bharat Kosh has, through private contributions by individuals, companies and institutions, already collected and released over Rs 1,000 crore (~ $150 million) for specific sanitation projects. Several private companies have directly implemented swachhata projects through their corporate social responsibility (CSR) programmes, especially in villages surrounding their factory premises, and in schools. Additionally, all the Ministries and Departments of the Government of India have mainstreamed sanitation in their respective sectors.

They committed large sums of money from their own budgets for swachhata, amounting to over Rs 30,000 crore for the years 2017–18 and 2018–19.

To put it in a nutshell, India backed its big goal with big money. And the cross sectoral benefits have already begun to show. In 2017, UNICEF calculated that every rural family in an open defecation-free village in India saves an average of Rs 50,000 per year on account of reduced medical expenses, time saved and lives saved. They also pegged the return on investment for sanitation in India at over 400 per cent. The World Health Organization has said that India will have saved over 3 lakh lives by the time we become an ODF nation in 2019. A study by the Bill & Melinda Gates Foundation found that the number of children with diarrhoea and worms in their stool was 32 per cent and 44 per cent less respectively in ODF villages than in non-ODF villages in India. The number of stunted and wasted children is also 15 per cent and 37 per cent less in ODF villages as compared to non-ODF ones. In 2019, UNICEF estimated that an ODF village was almost 11.25 times less likely to have its groundwater sources contaminated. But probably the most significant outcome of SBM is the positive effect it has had on various other sectors of development and corresponding Government programmes. It is already increasing the effectiveness of the Integrated Child Development Services and the Beti Bachao Beti Padhao initiative by improving the nutrition intake capacity of children, and will enhance the productive potential of India's next generation of young people, adding tailwinds to programmes like Skill India and Make in India, among others.

SBM has fostered a thriving sanitation ecosystem, creating market opportunities for crores of skilled and unskilled labourers, and has also thrown up entrepreneurship opportunities across the country. According to a report published by the Toilet Board Coalition in 2017, the sanitation industry in India was estimated at approximately $32 billion, and set to increase to $62 billion by 2021. These figures are augmented by a number of factors like job creation, increased demand and supply of sanitation equipment and systems, recycling of sanitation waste, etc. The massive improvement in the sanitation coverage of India has resulted in direct employment opportunities for masons, labourers and industries involved in supplying sanitary ware, as well as for associated sectors like cement, bricks, etc. On an average, building a toilet requires one mason and two labourers to work for three days, nine person days of work. For construction of the over 9 crore toilets so far under SBM, over 80 crore person days of employment has been generated. If one person-year of work comprises 200 working days, this comes to over 40 lakh person years of work – a full-time job for 40 lakh people for a year each. An average twin-pit toilet needs approximately 1,000 bricks to construct. This means toilets under SBM-G have used over 9,000 crore bricks! Approximately 100 kg of cement is used per toilet, meaning toilets under SBM have resulted in the use of over 90 lakh tonnes of cement.

While the construction of toilets has had massive implications for the economy, their maintenance, repair and retrofitting will continue to be a major chunk of the market. As aspirations grow, people will want to further upgrade their toilets, and also add bathing facilities. The Toilet Board Coalition also estimates that once households have a toilet, they spend another 52 per cent of the cost of the original toilet on upgrades and accessories over time.

This enormous sanitation ecosystem has created a huge opportunity for banks and financial institutions as well to finance individuals and communities that are borrowing to build personal or community-level infrastructure for solid and liquid management and water over and above the Government funding. To further promote easy borrowing for sanitation, the Ministry of Finance is working with the Ministry of Drinking Water and Sanitation to devise a Swachh Credit scheme, which will provide simple and easy-to-process sanitation loans to individuals and communities, and especially to sanitation entrepreneurs looking to convert waste to wealth in the fields of solid waste collection and management, faecal sludge management, and recycling and reuse of greywater.

Guided by unwavering political leadership, strengthened by cross-sectoral partnerships and driven by massive people's participation, the engines of SBM have been fuelled by public financing. The Mission's achievements make each and every Indian proud. Nowhere in the world has such a large population been mobilized to bring about such massive behaviour change in such a short span of time. India has now become the global leader of the war against open defecation, with several countries wanting to learn from our experience and implement similar programmes in their countries. What started off as a surprise announcement on Independence Day five years ago has spiralled into the biggest jan andolan in independent India.

SBM and the Circular Sanitation Economy

CHERYL HICKS

Chief Executive Officer, Toilet Board Coalition

THE ACHIEVEMENTS OF the Swachh Bharat Mission (SBM) provide impressive and inspiring evidence of how transformation can happen with speed and create an immediate positive impact, improving the lives of millions of people. In particular, the positively disruptive approaches of the Government of India (GoI) of targeting the status quo by engaging young people, the media and influencers; embracing new ideas, making sanitation everyone's business; and setting a sunset clause deadline for scale up in only five years have been instrumental in the Mission's success.

At the Toilet Board Coalition, a private sector platform focused on business solutions for sanitation, we see a parallel opportunity for the transformation of the economics of sanitation – from unaffordable public costs to sustainable and resilient systems via scale up of the Sanitation Economy. As SBM moves into the next phase, business has a new and important role to play in partnership with the Central and state governments to ensure the success of an Open Defecation Free (ODF) India.

In addition to a revolutionary behaviour change campaign, SBM has also been a monumental market-building campaign, stimulating industries, innovation, and entrepreneurship and paving the way for the growth of new sectors and supply chains in the Sanitation Economy. The investment the GoI has made in ending open defecation and ensuring access to sanitation for all is, in a way, returnable capital.

The Sanitation Economy is estimated to be a $32 billion a year market and set to double at $62 billion annually in India by 2021 (Toilet Board Coalition, 2017), creating many new jobs – even in the most rural areas of the country – reducing health and environmental costs and creating savings for households. Many toilet and related hardware suppliers have reported boosted sales during the SBM period, and they project recurring sales via toilet upgrades, establishing that people are willing to pay for sanitation. The post-ODF environment is creating new demand for faecal sludge management (FSM), solid waste management, organic and plastic waste solutions – all being cost-recoverable and revenue-generating solutions via the Circular Sanitation Economy. The management information system created to track the progress of SBM is another unique and positive outcome. This information is invaluable for businesses as it indicates potential new market development areas. Digitizing sanitation presents new opportunities to create Sanitation Intelligence, by transforming sanitation systems into smart toilets with smart treatment and information that enables smart preventative health.

Inspired by the success factors of the SBM campaign, this essay applies these successful SBM approaches to the opportunity to scale up the Sanitation Economy in India 2019–25.

Disrupting the Status Quo: Creating Demand for Sanitation Economy Solutions for Post-SBM India

The status quo view on sanitation is that 'providing sanitation is the responsibility of governments and is an inevitable cost to society'.

Just as demonstrated by SBM, the Sanitation Economy presents an alternative view: there is an enormous amount of value in our sanitation systems that has been left virtually untapped; that the private sector is increasingly playing a new and important role in bringing innovative solutions to the sector; and that there is commercial investment interest in profit-making business models in the sector.

Innovative businesses and entrepreneurs are disrupting the status quo of sanitation delivery by focusing on the creation of value, engaging young people and embracing new ideas. Leveraging the expertise of large companies as well as working together with local entrepreneurs is enabling the scale up of economically viable solutions. Business is bringing new thinking to the sector, from circular economy digitization to pay-as-you-go solar.

The Sanitation Economy transforms the economics of sanitation into a net positive value proposition for both businesses and governments, over and above the social benefits it accrues. Sanitation Economy systems are based on cost recovery and revenue generation by identifying new value – social, environmental and economic – in the system that can be monetized for sustainability and resilience.

In this model, the public sector benefits from private sector expertise, and the private sector sustainably engages in the development agenda through relevant, appropriate commercial constructs. This means focusing on scale or scalable projects, establishing streamlined go-to-market models, and creating favourable economics that attract investment.

Quick Wins Reinforce Belief: Supply of Scalable Business Solutions Are Available Today

Since 2015, leading businesses of the Toilet Board Coalition (Unilever, Kimberly-Clark, LIXIL, Firmenich, Tata, Veolia) and a growing sector of innovators have been building the Sanitation Economy. New economic evidence and business models, and product and service providers are now available for scale in India, providing pathways to the sustainability and resilience of SBM's achievements.

There is now a growing pipeline of businesses globally, with significant growth, creating innovative products for the Sanitation Economy and becoming service providers in rural communities and cities in India. Some of these are public toilet models; household toilet products and services, feminine care products, and waste management models generating water, energy and fertilizer. Sanitation health sensors generate new data and insights about human health and behaviour, including infectious disease monitoring.

These quick wins demonstrated over the past few years can be utilized to reinforce everyone's belief and further disrupt the status quo.

The work of the Toilet Board Coalition and its members has revealed that, on average, per 1 million people served, countries can gain $70 million in increased productivity through the provision of safe sanitation. In addition, every $1 invested sees a return of investment of $5 in positive externalities – including healthcare services and increased attendance at schools. Decentralized sanitation solutions, which are 5x more affordable than sewers, demonstrate that waste-water management can be done at a much lower cost. Through these we can save 2.6 billion litres of water per year; treat 65,000 tonnes of sanitation waste, or 'toilet resources', per year that would have otherwise polluted the environment and caused tremendous public health risk; produce more than 19,000 tonnes of organic fertilizer and help local farmers gain access to increased supply of affordable agricultural inputs, thereby increasing yields and incomes while addressing food security issues.

SBM has built 97 million toilets since 2 October 2014. These household toilets could produce approximately 50 million tonnes of toilet resources per year which can be treated to become: 490 billion

MJ of briquettes, 101 billion MJ of biogas or 7 million tonnes of compost.[1]

Remaining Fearless: Requiring Companies to Raise the Bar on Safely Managed Sanitation in Operations for Scale

Many businesses believe that sanitation is a development issue and not a mainstream business issue. But sanitation is every business's business. Poorly managed sanitation has become a business risk that has far-reaching effects – including on the health of workers and customers, their families and communities, their well-being and productivity, the environmental contamination of soil and water, and climate change via methane emissions.

Businesses are responsible for their employees and the communities in which they operate. Every company's responsibility must include ensuring safely managed sanitation for all, and via Sanitation Economy, these solutions would no longer mean unrecoverable costs for businesses.

Scaling up safely managed sanitation, and lower-cost/cost-recovery solutions will require the transformation of sanitation from a developmental issue alone to a mainstream business issue. That goes beyond corporate social responsibility to ensuring sanitation access for employees; to understanding the risks of poorly managed sanitation for business; and to the new business opportunities of the Sanitation Economy.

---

1 Estimations based on the Toilet Board Coalition's toilet calculator piloted via a 2018 demonstration project on tea plantations in Assam. It seeks to provide governments, businesses and cities with an assessment of economic, environmental and social benefits of different circular sanitation solutions.

Unleashing the Influencers: Financing Sustainable and Resilient Sanitation Systems via the Sanitation Economy

Just as the media was a key influencer in the success of SBM, finance and financial actors can influence the scale up of the Sanitation Economy. Emergent Sanitation Economy sectors remain high risk for investors as business models are new and may lack a sound financial track record. However, many innovative investment initiatives are under development and are coming online to support the sector, and provide incentives for investors and more robust financial data that investors require.

Catalytic capital, additional credit, microfinance, blended finance models and bringing safely managed sanitation into company ratings for investors are all needed. Some promising new financing options can be advocated by governments to better finance Sanitation Economy sectors.

1. *Addressing the Pioneering Gap – Catalytic Capital – Development Impact Bonds*

The growing interest in outcome-based funding among some of the biggest development funders represents an opportunity for impact-focused investors to participate in new sanitation solutions that have until recently been seen as too complex and high risk.

Development Impact Bonds (DIBs) are performance-based investment instruments intended to finance development outcomes in low-resource countries. This model maximizes the benefits of private enterprise – the focus on reducing costs, delivering quality service on an ongoing basis and generating revenue – while also recognizing that sanitation is not yet a purely commercial market, and that catalytic capital is needed to make the market work for all.

DIBs combine (i) Contingent funding of impact by donors against a pre-agreed set of outcomes metrics; (ii) External commercial investors who provide pre-financing for an intervention and take on the risk of under-performance; and (iii) A contractual framework that incentivizes frontline service providers to track progress and adapt the intervention as it proceeds, to maximize the likelihood of success.

2. *Incentives for Investors – Additional Credit into the Market – Risk Guarantee Facilities*

Guarantees are an effective instrument to mobilize commercial financing for development outcomes. Guarantee facilities enable financial institutions to finance small- and medium-sized enterprises (SMEs) whose investments ensure sustainable growth and development in low-income economies. In addition, these facilities have the potential to create employment through the SMEs accessing financing.

Guarantees can take on different forms, for example, loan guarantees, equity guarantees, fundraising guarantees, payment guarantees, etc.

3. *More Robust Financial Data – Bringing Safely Managed Sanitation into Company Ratings for Investors*

Since 1999, the creation of corporate disclosure data, assessing the risks and management of sustainable development issues on companies' long-term financial value via ratings and disclosure mechanisms has become an expectation of investors.

This information initially focused on carbon and climate risk but has since moved on to water and other sustainable development risks for business. Investors have determined that sustainability factors represent opportunities and risks that competitive companies must address. Sustainability-related mega-trends are changing our world and are having a measurable impact on companies' top and bottom lines. The quality of a company's strategy and management and its performance in dealing with opportunities and risks deriving from economic, environmental and social developments can be quantified and used to identify and select leading companies for investment purposes.

Requiring disclosure on access to sanitation and safely managed sanitation services by companies for the communities that operate in would influence more companies to consider their risks, creating more demand and data for business solutions, required by investors.

Sunset Clause (2025): Setting an Ambitious Deadline to Scale Up the Sanitation Economy in India for Sustained Economic Growth

Learning from the success of SBM, setting an ambitious deadline achieves results. The Sanitation Economy, as described in this essay, presents the opportunity to transform the economics of sanitation by engaging the private sector to ensure systems sustainability and resilience. There are many positive steps that the Government can take to enable the Sanitation Economy to thrive, including advocating the benefits of business solutions for sanitation, and working in partnership with the private sector to create conducive policy enabling environments for business solutions to scale.

Some of these include formalizing reinvented toilet products and services that enable resource recovery (such as FSM), and data recovery (such as public health data); regulations to control safety standards related to new products, resources, data and services of the Sanitation Economy; skills development and promotion of innovation and sanitation entrepreneurship, private sector value chains; public procurement policies that encourage Sanitation Economy solutions; and shared responsibility between the Government and the private sector.

The Government of India has emerged as a global leader in the sanitation revolution needed to achieve Sustainable Development

Goal 6. It is well positioned to lead the global transition to the Sanitation Economy, which presents significant potential for economic growth, transforming the economics of sanitation from unaffordable public costs to sustainable business opportunities, while improving billions of lives.

Good Sanitation Is Good Economics: Challenges and Solutions

HARTWIG SCHAFER

Regional Vice President, World Bank

IMAGINE WAKING UP tomorrow without access to sanitation. No toilet to use. No pipes to take away the waste or any system in place for that waste to be treated. And imagine having no sink or soap for washing your hands.

Hard to envision, isn't it? Yet this is a daily reality for far too many people: according to UNICEF and World Health Organization's (WHO) Joint Monitoring Program, two billion people still did not have basic sanitation facilities such as toilets or latrines in 2017, and of these, 673 million defecated in the open.

All too often with such stark statistics, their scale numbs us to the personal toll inflicted. That figure of two billion means that one out of every 3.5 people on the planet – mothers, daughters, sisters and wives; fathers, sons, brothers and husbands – were denied the basic safety, dignity and opportunity of sanitation.

This is why the ambitious Sustainable Development Goal (SDG) 6.2 calls for ensuring universal access to safe sanitation services by

2030. Although impressive progress has been made in recent years, throughout much of the developing world achieving this goal remains a fundamental challenge. Ensuring universal access to safe sanitation services requires not only the provision of sanitation infrastructure, but also the containment of waste and its safe conveyance, treatment and disposal. The successful implementation of these interventions at scale, as we have learned from India's Swachh Bharat Mission (SBM), is possible only with sound political will, solid public finance, strong policies and sustained people engagement to achieve long-term behaviour change.

Why Sanitation Matters

The Government of India launched SBM in 2014 because it understood the compelling economic and social reasons that justified giving priority to addressing the challenge of sanitation access across the country. The World Bank has also realized that, beyond the human dignity aspects of ensuring the availability of safe sanitation facilities to all, there is a conspicuous link between access to improved sanitation and improved human development outcomes. The World Bank's Human Capital Index illustrates the effects that improved sanitation has on human development outcomes (Gatti et al. 2018; Figure 1). While the figure below does not imply a causal relationship, it convincingly demonstrates that as sanitation improves, the Human Capital Index also increases. While none of the indicators which comprise the Human Capital Index, such as health and education, explicitly includes water and sanitation, the graph clearly shows that sanitation underlies and impacts them all. As such, the World Bank realizes that sanitation can accentuate and accelerate human capital, which in turn drives economic growth, helping us tackle extreme poverty and create more inclusive societies.

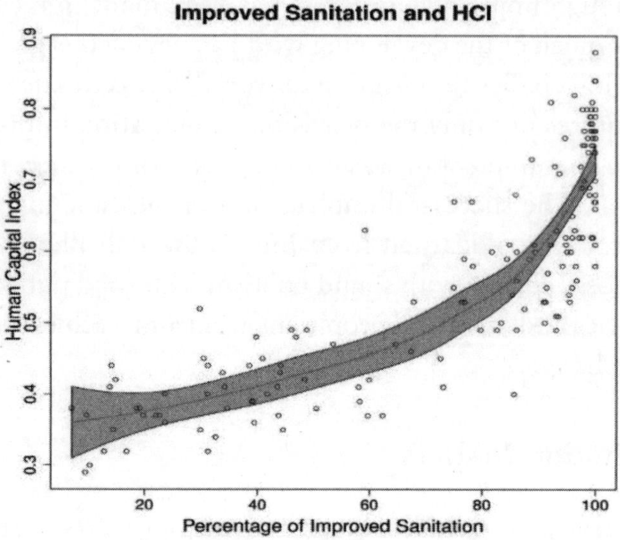

Figure 1: The Relationship between Improved Sanitation and the Human Capital Index

Notes: Human Capital Index (Gatti et al. 2018); Improved sanitation (https://washdata.org/). R square values for linear regression models are: 0.6898. Source: Authors' calculations. Each dot signifies a country included in the Human Capital Project of the World Bank.

Good Sanitation Is Good Economics

A large body of evidence documents why this is the case. Poor sanitation alone kills nearly 9,00,000 people per year, or around 2,460 people every day. Tragically, 56 per cent of deaths of children under the age of five are due to diarrhoea which is related to poor sanitation. Even those who survive its pernicious impacts are not spared: poor sanitation can also make people sick. For adults, it means higher health expenditures, lower productivity and reduced wages. In many countries, poor sanitation can trap households in a vicious cycle of poverty. For children, it limits their ability to absorb nutrients and imperils their physical and cognitive development, denying them the ability to accumulate human capital, and grow into healthy, productive and smart adults who can contribute more to the economy and fulfil their potential.

Girls are particularly affected. Without the privacy afforded by toilets they are more likely to drop out of school, and less likely to secure a job and participate in the economy in later life. Examples of interventions that explicitly target and reduce community levels of open defecation, such as in rural Mali, show significant effects on reducing under-five stunting (Pickering et al. 2015).

Investments in good sanitation provide some of the largest development dividends for an economy. The WHO reports that the economic return on sanitation spending is $5.50 for every $1 invested – as a Return on Investment that would be the envy of investment bankers everywhere. On the other hand, the costs of inaction are staggering. Every year, inadequate sanitation costs the world an estimated $260 billion. Clearly, investing in sanitation is an investment that pays dividends, now and in the future: the returns are high, the savings are big and the benefits to people can transform lives.

The Government of India, most notably through its pledge to end open defecation, recognizes these social and economic benefits. That's why they have made the eradication of open defecation a priority and mobilized almost $20 billion towards the nationwide mission that began in 2014. And this is also why the World Bank is contributing to the ambitious SBM with a $1.5 billion loan, one of its largest ever, and has helped introduce a performance-based approach that links funding directly to results in the expectation that hundreds of millions of Indians can wake up and make use of a clean and safe toilet within their household compound.

The World Bank has been delighted to partner with the Government of India on SBM as the lessons from its bold approach of providing political leadership and public finance to deliver a massive programme at scale are influencing the design of Bank programmes across the world. Improved sanitation also benefits sectors of the economy dependent on water quality, such as fisheries, agriculture and services. There are benefits to the environment, too, through lower levels of surface-water pollution and groundwater contamination. Moreover, there is growing evidence, including through case studies from Senegal and Sri Lanka, that large-scale government commitment and investment in sanitation for all across the sanitation ecosystem can spur growth and vitalize local economies, creating jobs for masons and small-scale contractors who build toilets; for construction material suppliers; and for social workers and mass media who implement programmes to deliver behaviour change at scale; for a whole new grassroots industry of service providers who will maintain sanitation facilities, manage and treat septage and ensure its safe disposal into the environment.

In India, SBM has created and delivered on this opportunity for entrepreneurship at scale. The Mission has trained women across rural India and they have eagerly stepped up to become masons and increase their earning opportunities by constructing toilets (Women's Leadership in SBM-Grameen, World Bank 2018, p. 8).

Addressing Sanitation Challenges

There is no single solution to the sanitation challenge; however, ensuring the availability of toilets at home and in public buildings is a necessary step in the development of a sanitation service chain.

Changing Mindsets

Better health and other economic impacts of access to sanitation facilities can be achieved only by the effective and sustainable use of these facilities by all members of the population. One of the lessons the World Bank has learned, not only from SBM, but also from our projects across several countries, is that it's not just about building a toilet – it's about changing the mindsets and encouraging people to use them. Achieving lasting behaviour and social change remains essential to sustaining the development outcomes of improved sanitation. This means tackling those 'below the waterline' elements of change – breaking taboos and addressing biases. After all, changing centuries-old habits of defecating in the open is a complex undertaking involving behaviour change at a deep level. Yet, examples from around the world and from SBM have shown that community-led sanitation programmes can and do change people's behaviour around sanitation. By entrusting and empowering households and communities and building ownership around the cause of becoming open defecation free, these programmes may sustain achievements in sanitation with lasting impacts.

SBM has placed considerable emphasis on behaviour change campaigns at all levels and utilized many different channels and platforms to do so. Importantly, it provides opportunities for women to take leading roles in their communities. Women comprise roughly 30-40 per cent of the volunteers – swachhagrahis – who lead the process of triggering behaviour change at the village level (World Bank 2018, pg. 1). In addition, enlisting well-known celebrities and mass media has proven to be an effective means of disseminating important messages. The Darwaza Band mass media campaigns supported by the World Bank focus on 'closing the door' on open defecation and sustaining behaviour change as a community.

Toilets Alone Are Not Enough

While building household toilets outside of each home provides every family member access to a dignified service, pit latrines and septic tanks do fill up, and their waste must be treated, just like any piped sewage system. An analysis of data from 39 countries shows that 43 per cent of the human waste that is transmitted through sewers is untreated. Similarly, the sewer-connected toilet is not the right fit for every community. Such toilets require significant amounts of water and well-functioning sewer infrastructure to operate effectively. At the same time, in the absence of sewer-connected toilets, people around the world use a range of non-sewered, on-site toilet options to meet their needs. While these options safely contain human waste, they need to be linked to collection and treatment systems that ensure the removal of pathogens from the environment. The twin-pit toilets being promoted by SBM are an important and innovative technology that manages the waste on-site and also requires less water.

There are also huge opportunities for effective resource recovery – by generating energy and nutrient-rich by-products from treated waste, and re-using these for agriculture, or even the production of recycled or 'new' water. All of this requires creativity, technological innovation and novel ways of delivering services across the value chain – which in turn create jobs and opportunities.

Finance, Incentives and Institutions

Breakthroughs in financing models are also needed to provide sanitation as a service which responds to user demands. To this end, setting clear public policy goals and using public funds to leverage the financing and technical capabilities of the private sector, as demonstrated by SBM, are critical to accelerate the integration of disruptive thinking and the adoption of innovative approaches to deliver sanitation solutions at scale.

Several countries are implementing these ideas. In Sri Lanka, for example, the National Water Supply and Drainage Board is testing a new model of public–private partnerships for toilet improvement and septage management in four municipalities outside of Colombo. In India, large public investments in sanitation have been instrumental in building momentum for improving sanitation across the country. These examples show that there is a fundamental complementarity between infrastructure and institutions, and both are central to improving the quality of sanitation in the developing world (Ashraf, Glaeser and Ponzetto, 2016).

A Complex Challenge – But Not Insurmountable

Ultimately, investing in sanitation is about preventing needless deaths, investing in people and transforming lives. Achieving improved and safely managed sanitation for all may be a complex challenge, but the transition from open defecation to the safe disposal and treatment of waste is possible – and essential. Toilet-building combined with other factors such as social and behaviour change, maintenance and repair of toilets, waste and drainage management and treatment, re-use of by-products of treated waste for productive purposes, innovations in technology and finance along with institutional and policy reforms remain the key ingredients to help countries meet the challenge of sustained sanitation improvement.

Keeping an Eye on the Ball: Measuring Results and Impact

Global experience has highlighted the importance of effective monitoring and assessment mechanisms to measure the short- and long-term performance and impacts. The World Bank support to SBM builds such capacity at the national, state and gram panchayat levels. This includes annual monitoring of progress through a nation-wide survey, the National Annual Rural Sanitation Survey. This measures not only the availability of safe sanitation facilities, but also the sustained use of these facilities by the population. Such monitoring helps measure progress and informs when course correction may be required. Two rounds of this survey have been completed, the first in 2017–18 and the second in 2018–19, and they have shown the significant progress India has made in increasing access to sanitation in a short span of time. The World Bank is committed to supporting the Government of India in continuing these surveys to ensure that sustained and effective use is being made of the toilet facilities, so that the intended economic, social and environmental benefits of SDG 6.2 are fully realized.

Solutions to the challenge of attaining sustainable universal sanitation are available as demonstrated by the lessons and results of SBM. This is perhaps the right moment for other countries across the world to seize the momentum of SBM by providing the same level of political leadership and financing to achieve the SDG objectives of an open-defecation-free world. The World Bank is proud to support SBM and, through its Lighthouse India initiative, stands ready to build on the tremendous results of SBM and work with partners across the world to deliver a future where sound political leadership, public financing, policy direction and people's engagement ensure that the safety, dignity and opportunity of sanitation become a reality for all.

Comparison of the Costs and Benefits of the Clean India Mission

GUY HUTTON, NICOLAS OSBERT AND FRANCIS ODHIAMBO

UNICEF

SANITATION AND HYGIENE not only have major consequences for dignity, disease risk and the environment when not practised properly, they also cut to the very heart of economic development. The World Bank estimated the value of the impacts of inadequate sanitation in India equal to \$53 billion (Rs 2.4 trillion) in the year 2006, equivalent to 6.4 per cent of India's GDP in the same year (World Bank, 2011).

Prime Minister Narendra Modi launched the Swachh Bharat Mission (SBM) and announced on 2 October 2014 that India aimed to be Open Defecation Free (ODF) within five years. Given India's sheer size and diversity, this was an uphill task, unparalleled in history, making SBM the world's largest ever sanitation campaign. In 2015, 59 per cent of rural households and 12 per cent of urban households in India did not have a sanitary toilet, leaving 522 million people still practising open defecation nationally (World Health Organization and UNICEF, 2017).

In a study we (UNICEF) worked on in 2017, we measured the major costs and benefits of the campaign after three years of implementation to draw conclusions about its return on investment. Benefit-cost model inputs were obtained from household surveys in the twelve largest Indian states where open defecation was practised at the time, along with drawing on other national surveys and research literature. Costs included household and Government investments and household operational costs for the toilet and handwashing facility. Benefits included reductions in medical costs and mortality associated with diarrhoeal diseases, productive time saved from fewer diarrhoea cases and having to find a place to defecate, and an increase in the value of property.

A tailored household survey for the purposes of this study was implemented in rural households across 12 states from 20 July to 11 August 2017. The final sample frame consisted of 1,57,853 villages from 2,317 blocks across the states.

The study showed the interventions under SBM are highly cost-beneficial: annual benefits of $727 (approximately Rs 50,000) per household are from health-related savings (55 per cent) and from sanitation access time savings (45 per cent). Over 10 years, the benefit-cost ratio (BCR) – the number of times the overall benefits exceed the overall costs of sanitation across the selected households – is 1.7 (household financial perspective) and 4.0 (societal perspective), considering all costs and benefits with universal toilet use in ODF communities.

The Benefit-Cost Ratio

Cost-benefit analysis (CBA) was used to compare the costs and benefits of SBM's intervention with those had the households not built a private toilet. BCRs were presented under two scenarios, comparing those households with versus those without private toilets at home: (a) including only financial costs and financial benefits to households, in order to assess direct cash impact at the household level; and (b) including full societal costs and benefits, to understand how cost-beneficial the intervention is from the overall use of society's resources. Our study sought to answer whether investments in SBM over the period 2014–17 have been cost-beneficial to the households who built the toilets and to society at large, and to conclude how SBM can further enhance its gains.

Costs included both investment and operational costs for a household toilet and a handwashing station. It was recorded how these costs were financed, such as whether from Government-delivered hardware subsidies, resources provided by non-state actors or by the households themselves from their income, savings or a loan (as reported by the households). Costs included expenditures for behaviour change and social marketing activities, construction materials, paid labour, other fees as well as non-financial costs, which principally included household time investments in construction and maintenance. Operations and maintenance (O&M) costs such as soap, water, cleaning, pit emptying and repairs were included when reported by households, and estimated on an annual basis. Cost estimates were annualized assuming a ten-year lifespan of the toilet and adding O&M.

Benefits included were the health impact, the time use (time lost or saved in accessing toilets) and the increase in property value from construction and use of a household toilet. The impact on households' property value from having a toilet was estimated in consultation with the head of the household.

Meanwhile, health economic benefits were estimated assuming 47 per cent reduction in diarrhoeal morbidity and mortality from sanitation and hygiene interventions (Andres et al, 2014). In communities where the rate of toilet use was found to be less than 100 per cent – for instance, 85 per cent as found in the survey – the reduction in disease rates was estimated at 33 per cent (Andres et al, 2014). The morbidity benefits were monetized as the savings in medical costs incurred for the treatment of gastrointestinal diseases (doctor fees, laboratories, travel expenses, medications) and the savings in lost time of the patient and caretakers. Time saved was monetized at minimum wage rate under the national employment guarantee scheme for adults and half that wage rate for school-going children. The benefits from the reduced mortality rate were monetized using the value of a statistical life in India (Shanmugam, 2011).

Annual benefits of having and using a household latrine under SBM were estimated by summing the annual value of health and time savings, and then adding the estimated property value rise reported by the chief wage earner at the end of the ten-year period.

Results

Benefits

The annual benefits from health and time savings equal $727 (Rs 50,000) per household per year. Figure 1 shows that overall a significant share (55 per cent) of the annual benefits are from health savings with the rest (45 per cent) being sanitation access time savings. The average medical cost per episode of diarrhoeal diseases at any type of health facility was $63, which is saved when an episode was averted. The average duration of an illness episode was 1.8 days with an average 1.34 health facility visits per case. Of the savings in lost time in illness and caretaking, 52 per cent of the value accrued to the patient and 48 per cent to the caregiver. Substantial health benefits were due to the reductions in premature death, valued at $249 per year per household. The value of time savings – notably for accessing a toilet located by the house – is on average $325 per household per year. While only a proportion of time savings is likely to be used for income-generating activities, saved time still has value and can be used for things such as school work, subsistence activities and leisure; hence the contributions of a household toilet to the household economy are potentially significant.

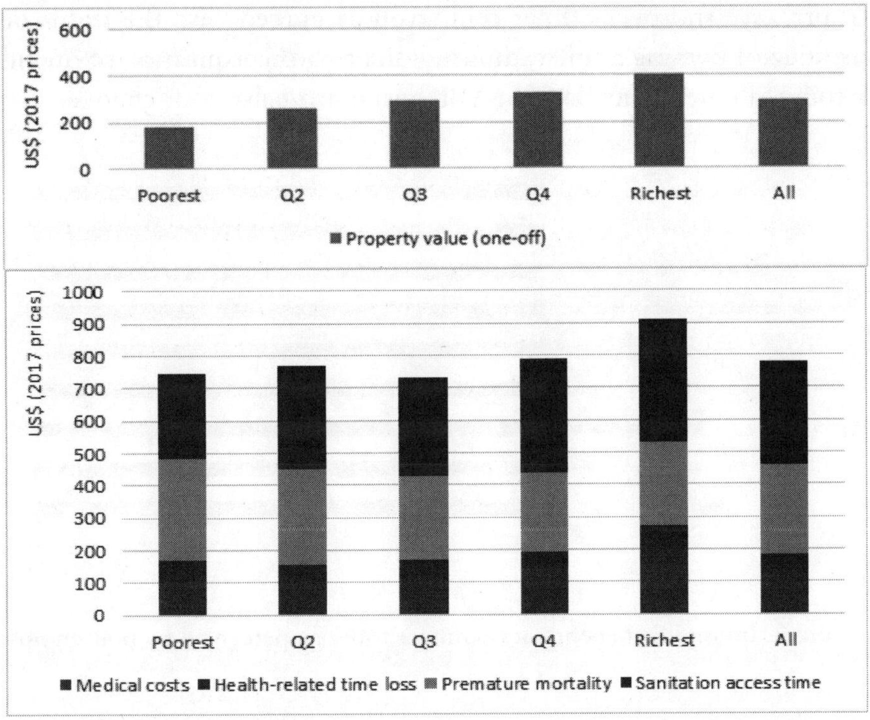

Figure 1. Annual benefits (below) and one-off benefits (above) of owning and using a latrine and handwashing station

The investment in a toilet is perceived to contribute positively to the value of the property, with an average rise in property value of $294, which is about 5 per cent of the reported property value of the house.

Intangible Social Benefits

Figure 2 indicates that there is an overwhelmingly positive response on the intangible benefits of having an improved household toilet. At least 80 per cent of households strongly agreed with the convenience benefits of a toilet (e.g. for menstruating women, for the elderly, during rainy periods); over 85 per cent strongly agreed that it is safer for girls and women; 85 per cent strongly agreed with the benefit of privacy; and over 80 per cent strongly agreed with the status or prestige of owning a toilet, thus highlighting the aspiration of owing a toilet, a core principle of SBM focusing on behaviour change.

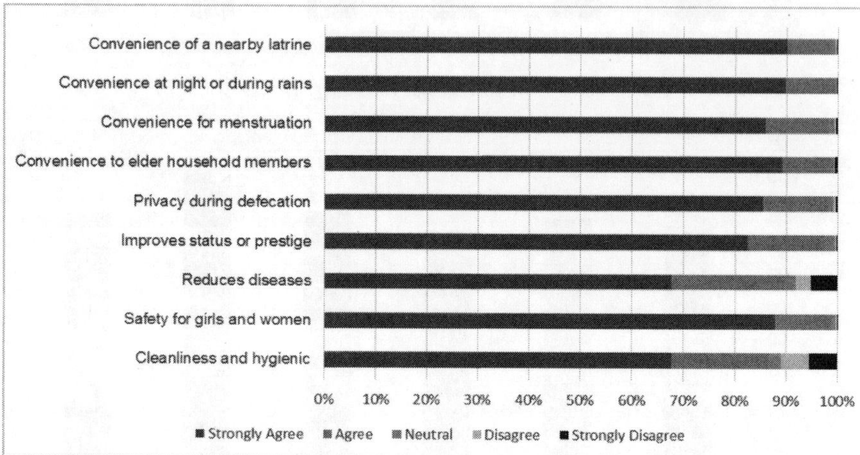

Figure 2. Intangible benefits of owning a toilet as perceived by households

Costs versus benefits

The BCR under the household financial perspective is 1.7 when toilet usage is 100 per cent, reducing to 1.1 at 85 per cent toilet use. Under the societal perspective, the benefits exceed costs four times (for 100 per cent toilet use) and three times (for 85 per cent toilet use). SBM's benefits are equitable from the societal perspective as the BCRs are higher for poorer households. For the poorest households, the BCR is 5.7 for households in ODF communities and 4.2 times for households in non-ODF communities.

Other economic measures shed further light on the performance of the intervention. The overall population-level annual rate of return on the financial investment is 31 per cent, which is well above what households would earn from putting their money into a bank savings account. For the poorest households, the financial annual rate of return is higher at 65 per cent. The net financial return on the household expenditure on the toilet and handwashing station (total benefit minus total cost over ten years) averages $296. The average payback period for the household financial investment is two years for all households, and one year for poorer households.

When the average lifespan of a toilet was increased from ten years in the base case to twenty years in an alternative scenario – a reasonable assumption for the households owning a twin-leach-pit toilet (63.6 per cent of sampled households), and the model promoted under SBM – the financial BCR increases to 2.1 and the societal BCR increases to 4.4.

Conclusions

This study has shown that the sanitation and hygiene interventions adopted under SBM resulted in major increases in new toilet ownership and usage, and are highly cost-beneficial in rural India, more particularly for the poorest households. *Investments in sanitation deliver a high return, both from household and societal perspectives, and deserve prioritized contributions from public funds.*

When interpreting these results, it should be understood that the value of benefits can be significantly greater than the estimates in this present study as several potential benefits were not included: sanitation value chain (e.g. reuse value of urine and excreta as compost and/or energy), tourism value and improvement in water quality. Moreover, social benefits were assessed qualitatively in the study, which indicated there are many beneficial social impacts of owning and using a toilet, over and above the health and time savings (Figure 2). However, even with the limited set of benefits and costs included in this analysis, the study findings strongly justify investments in sanitation and hygiene.

The study also indicates that the impact of SBM is dependent on the extent to which the entire community adopts sanitation and hygiene practices, and the sustainability of both the infrastructure and behaviours.

The most recent household survey on sanitation, the National Annual Rural Sanitation Survey (NARSS) 2018-19, conducted by an independent verification agency under the World Bank support project to the SBM-Grameen, has found that 96.5 per cent households in rural India who have access to a toilet use it. While these figures are reassuring, efforts are needed to sustain the intervention from both hardware (physical infrastructure) and software (behaviour change) perspectives. Indeed, UNICEF field experience globally shows compelling evidence that it takes time to achieve and sustain behaviour change for toilet usage to become a social norm.

For the past twelve months, anticipating this issue, the Government of India and its partners, including UNICEF, have been working on an 'ODF Plus' phase of the sanitation programme, looking at ODF-Sustainability through: continuous behaviour change, leaving no one behind/reaching universal access, retrofitting toilet technologies (the study found that about two-thirds of households had a twin-pit and most of the remaining had a septic tank), and solid and liquid waste management.

This phase is crucial to make the best of this unprecedented sanitation drive. Key stakeholders must remain fully mobilized and adequately funded for the full returns on investment to be enjoyed.

Considering the significant financial investments, the high level of political leadership, the people's participation including that of children (as the campaign was developed as a people's movement, a jan andolan), the broad partnerships, notably with academia, the private sector and development partners, SBM is an inspiring and impactful model of Sustainable Development Goals in action. Such programmes are critical to meet health-, education-, gender- and environment-related objectives.

For the full report on this study (UNICEF, 2018): http://unicef.in/Uploads/Publications/Resources/pub_doc20172.PDF

Sanitation Technology Innovations

BINDESHWAR PATHAK

Founder, Sulabh Sanitation Movement

ANCIENT SCRIPTURES FROM the Vedic period (1500–500 BCE) exhibit some practices developed for the safe disposal of solid waste and human waste. Over centuries, while sections of society worked towards the safe disposal of solid waste and cleaning, a sizeable population simply defecated in the open. While defecation in the open must have started during the Puranic period (200 BCE–500 CE), defecation near human habitations was prohibited on religious grounds. The ancient text of the Devi Purana tells the people to go some distance from their dwelling, dig a small pit, put some grass and leaves in it, and after defecation again put some grass and leaves and fill the pit with soil. A more or less similar situation continued in the centuries that followed.

During the British period, however, in the houses of the rulers and the rich, commodes replaced the bucket toilets and, in 1870, the British introduced the sewerage system in Calcutta for the disposal of human waste. Very costly in construction and maintenance, the sewerage system also required enormous quantities of water to flush. The other technology – septic tanks – was also costly in terms of construction and maintenance, and required 10 litres of water to flush per use.

The beginning of the twentieth century, however, brought forward a true visionary of the time: Mahatma Gandhi, who, for the first time, emphasized the need for local and decentralized, yet technical, arrangements for the safe disposal of human excreta. Gandhi said: 'No one should clean and carry human excreta of others just to earn one's livelihood. There must be some scientific method of human waste disposal.' Till such an invention was made, he suggested the use of trench latrines and putting soil over human excreta after defecation (*Tatti pe mitti*). His followers practised this but, of course, it was not a scalable, sustainable solution.

After Gandhi, many attempts were made by official and non-official organizations to improve the state of sanitation in the country. The Central and state Governments constituted many committees and commissions – Barve Committee, Malkani Committee, Kaka Kalelkar Commission, etc. – but none was able to make any concrete suggestions for decentralized and locally appropriate technical arrangements for safe sanitation.

In 1968, I joined the Bihar Gandhi Centenary Celebration Committee as a social worker. I read Gandhi's autobiography and other books related to him, which profoundly impacted me. The Centenary Committee had taken up numerous programmes, one of which was to restore the human rights and dignity of manual scavengers, who used to clean human excreta manually, carrying it as headload for disposal. Later, I learnt that this subhuman practice stemmed from the genesis of untouchability and had been continuing for almost 5,000 years.

Troubled by the pathetic conditions of manual scavengers and inspired by Gandhi's teachings, I realized that a suitable toilet technology was needed to solve the problems of open defecation as well as manual scavenging. So I put my head down and worked hard to devise a technology that could replace dry latrines and end the problem of cleaning bucket toilets and dry pit toilets once and for all.

My goal, thus, was not only to get a technological solution but also to liberate society from its long-held caste-based discriminations against manual scavengers. In 1968, I resolved to free this section of society from the shackles of slavery and dedicated my life to this cause. Soon after, in the early 1970s, I succeeded in inventing the twin-pit pour-flush ecological toilet technology (Sulabh Shauchalaya), which could replace bucket toilets that need manual intervention for cleaning them.

When I started the sanitation movement, houses in rural areas didn't have any toilets and everyone went out to defecate. The situation was equally bad in urban areas as well. More than 85 per cent houses had bucket toilets. In slums and on the outskirts of towns and cities, people practised open defecation. There was no provision of public toilets near railway stations, market yards, bus stops, and religious and tourist places. Foreigners who visited and travelled to India faced huge difficulties.

Gandhi's dream of a 'clean India' remained dormant until 2014, when Shri Narendra Modi took over as Prime Minister and brought sanitation to the centre stage. Laying Gandhian emphasis on sanitation, he launched the Swachh Bharat Mission and led an effective campaign to make India Open Defecation Free by 2019. What Gandhi had done in 1901, the Prime Minister did in 2014 when he took up a broom and started cleaning the streets of Delhi. This personal example that he set has ignited the people's minds, inspiring them to clean the streets, roads, offices and other public places.

The Sulabh twin-pit technology that I invented became an enabling tool in reducing open defecation in the villages. My journey began in 1973 from the Arrah Municipal Corporation in Bihar, where two Sulabh toilets were constructed for demonstration and usage. Subsequently, the Bihar Government accepted my technology. Since then, we have built 15 lakh Sulabh toilets in individual houses across the country. Now, rural women can relieve themselves with dignity, in the confines of their toilets. The same technology in schools has helped increase student attendance, especially of girls, and reduce the mortality rates in these areas.

The beauty of the Sulabh technology is that human excreta is converted into fertilizer as, out of the two pits, one is used at a time and the other remains a standby. When one pit is full, the faecal material is diverted to the second pit while the contents of the filled pit decompose into organic manure. The manual cleaning of human excreta is not required in this system. Besides, bio-fertilizer produced can be used to raise farm productivity. This technology proved to be the solution to the problems of open defecation and manual cleaning of excreta. It is affordable, indigenous and culturally acceptable, and has made an incredible impact. It has been widely accepted as the best suited toilet technology for rural areas as it is sustainable, easy to construct and requires no manual intervention for waste management.

Recognizing the technology as appropriate for rural areas, the Ministry of Drinking Water and Sanitation also adopted it and used a multipronged communication strategy to popularize it. Masons across districts have been trained in the construction of twin-pit toilets. They work in villages to promote this technology, particularly its ease of construction. In Jharkhand, a unique cadre of women masons called Rani Mistris are constructing twin-pit toilets with ease. Jharkhand's Rani Mistris have become champions of this technology across the country today.

Through the efforts of the Ministry, state governments and others, people have realized that the twin-pit toilet is easy to construct, easy to operate and maintain, and can be used on a sustainable basis. The efforts of the Ministry towards demonstrating that a filled pit of twin toilet, which contains decomposed faeces, is safe to be emptied by households themselves went a long way in popularizing the technique. Film stars, celebrities, senior Government officials participated in pit-emptying exercises and demonstrated that a twin pit completely decomposes the faecal matter and is safe to handle.

Having improved India's sanitation situation, the twin-pit toilet technology is poised for application in Asia, Africa and Latin America, for the nearly 230 crore people who have no access to hygienic toilets. Countries like India, Bangladesh, Vietnam, etc. have accepted the Sulabh technology. BBC Horizons has declared it 'one of five unique inventions of the world that has a direct bearing on humanity'. My low-cost and safe Sulabh Shauchalaya System has been implemented on a pan-Indian scale, and is an invention declared as a Global Best Practice by the United Nations Centre for Human Settlements. In 2000, the system received the Dubai International Award for best practices to improve the living environment. The United Nations Development Programme has recommended the adoption of Sulabh technology in its Human Development Report of 2003.

Another technology I developed is a biogas digester linked with public toilets. In this system, human excreta is passed through the digester for treatment. When decomposition takes place it produces biogas, which can be used for cooking, lighting mantle lamps and to generate electricity. The water discharged from the digester is treated with ultra-violet rays, making the water pure and safe to be discharged into river bodies or used as fertilizer. This technology can be adopted in housing colonies, schools, colleges, and hospitals where there is provision of a sewerage system. In the biogas digester, human excreta is fully recycled.

The Prime Minister's call for a Swachh Bharat has become a people's movement. Now everybody is paying attention to cleanliness, using dustbins and disposing dirt and waste materials properly. The heightened awareness about cleanliness is now so palpable that even children remind their parents not to throw anything on roads or in public spaces. The Prime Minister's call for a toilet in every household to stop open defecation has inspired people to recognize the need to have a sanitary toilet at home. Examples of popular enthusiasm for toilets abound. A hundred-year-old poor woman sold her goats and paid for building her household toilet. Now, marriageable girls persuade their parents to first check whether their potential in-laws' house has a toilet or not. Some of them ask for a toilet as a wedding gift instead of ornaments! As a result of all this, as of June 2019, toilet coverage in the country has crossed 96 per cent and India is on the verge of becoming an Open Defecation Free country.

The credit for bringing sanitation centre stage and making it a mass movement goes to the Prime Minister, Shri Narendra Modi. Making India clean and ending open defecation will make him immortal in the history of India. Credit for this monumental achievement is also due to Shri Parameswaran Iyer, Secretary, Ministry of Drinking Water and Sanitation, Government of India, and his team and officials at the Central and state levels who have been instrumental in the successful implementation of Swachh Bharat.

I would like to end this essay with what I earlier wrote about the Prime Minister and the Swachh Bharat Mission:

> Prime Minister Shri Narendra Modi has ignited the candle of cleanliness among Indians. He has inspired Indians to restore the culture of sanitation that our ancestors had during the Indus Valley civilization. We should join hands with the Prime Minister with all our strength and resources, to make India clean and free from open defecation. Be civilized, be cultured, be clean, make India clean and stand out in the front row of civilized, cultured and clean nations.

Sanitation Financing: Opportunities and Potential

GARY WHITE AND MATT DAMON

Founders, Water.org

THE SWACHH BHARAT Mission (SBM) is a story for our times: at once a bold public commitment, a grand people's movement, a large-scale behaviour change campaign, and a catalyst for broader forces of finance (households and self-help groups have taken out loans worth hundreds of crores to build toilets). It is not a story with one hero; it has more heroes than we can count. The scale of its success is documented throughout this book in truly staggering numbers.

The big picture of this achievement is amazing to reflect on, but for the moment let's not look at the big picture. Let's cut to the perspective of a single rural family. From here, the need for water and sanitation credit comes into focus.

The scene is like this: A woman with a family, living in an Indian village, wants a toilet. She knows that an incentive of Rs 12,000 is available under SBM to help her build one, and some of her neighbours have used this to install their first toilets.

However, she also knows that Rs 12,000 may not cover the whole cost of constructing her toilet – the toilet *she* aspires to build. She doesn't want a basic toilet; she wants a toilet that her family will use and look after for many years to come. It may cost more than what the incentive covers if she adds a bathing facility, and she knows she will only receive the incentive in full once she provides photos of the finished toilet. Even for a basic toilet, she needs start-up funds first – and for her this is difficult to mobilize immediately. And additional funds to build her dream toilet. She is caught in a gap. No matter how much she believes in the cause of Swachh Bharat to immediately construct a toilet, her family either has to go to a loan shark and risk falling into a debt trap or is left going out to the fields every morning until she can save enough money.

A Gap the Size of the Future

It is these small gaps at the household level that made the aspirations of a movement like Swachh Bharat even more challenging, in spite of the massive efforts undertaken by the Government of India to create awareness on the need for a toilet, change existing behaviours to end open defecation and support creation of infrastructure through a healthy incentive. Once we cut back to the big picture, and multiply this by potentially millions of households, these added up to a large challenge indeed.

Globally, achieving the first two targets of Sustainable Development Goal 6 on water – access to safe drinking water, and adequate and equitable sanitation and hygiene for all, including an end to open defecation – will require finances of about $114 billion every year up to 2030. How far are we from that? The gap in financing is still three times the total spending in the sector. And this severe shortfall has severe consequences. More than 2 billion people globally lack access to basic sanitation. Worldwide, women and girls spend 266 million hours every day finding a place to defecate. Every 90 seconds, a child dies of a waterborne disease.

In India, the incentives mobilized under SBM have worked wonders in helping bridge the gap and shift the numbers. Yet this public movement has been so successful precisely because it acknowledges that it is not acting alone. A variety of alternative sources of finance was critical to carry households the rest of the way across the gap. Such market-based solutions allow the Central and state governments to use every rupee of public funding right and targeted – incentivize sweeping behaviour change, enable a call to action and help the people most in need. Thus, quietly, alternative finance has become the other side of the incredible story of SBM.

Micro-lending in the Swachh Bharat Era

It is a story that the organization we founded, Water.org, has been living for more than two decades, though never on the scale achieved in India during the years of SBM.

We are deeply committed to helping households at the base of the economic pyramid solve their water and sanitation problems. To do this, we partner with and catalyse a diversity of financial institutions that can reach those households. When we began partnering with Indian microfinance institutions (MFIs) in 2008, progress was slow but steady. The MFIs were willing to be convinced that people would borrow money to get a water connection or to construct a toilet, and that those people would be able to repay the loan. But they did need convincing.

The launch of SBM changed everything. When a small loan from a financial institution is combined with an incentive from SBM, millions of households can easily borrow all or most of the start-up funds they needed to build the toilet of their dreams, and still be confident of repaying. The gap became much narrower. We realized what a powerful alignment this could be: an enormous public commitment and a historic popular movement committed to helping economically weaker sections of society realize their dream toilet, combined with civil society organizations and lenders who work with the households.

Realizing the potential, Water.org approached the Ministry of Drinking Water and Sanitation (MDWS) to work together to scale micro-lending for sanitation. When Prime Minister Narendra Modi launched the Swachh Bharat Mission to achieve an Open Defecation Free (ODF) India by 2019, he invited civil society, corporate businesses and individual citizens to partner with the Government to achieve this dream and assured support. MDWS has been a champion that quickly recognized the need for micro-loans and has supported Water.org to scale its efforts across the country. With MDWS leading the way, we have contributed to policy changes which incentivize lending for water and sanitation, partnered with Government agencies at the national and state levels and advocated to various financial institutions to create water and sanitation products. Overall, this partnership has helped make record progress in building the solutions to achieve sanitation for all.

How Is a Toilet Not Like a Luxury Car?

In particular, a few enablers have shaped the lending ecosystem to such an extent that we must give them a turn in the spotlight. The first of these has been Priority Sector Lending (PSL). Since the 1970s, PSL has powered financial inclusion in India by mandating banks to allocate 40 per cent of their lending to priority sectors. These have included vital necessities like housing and education – but not, for many decades, water or sanitation. Without priority sector allocation, a loan for a toilet would have to compete in the same arena as a loan for a luxury car. Banks were seldom interested. Then, in 2012, the Reserve Bank of India began re-examining the mandate of PSL. Water.org and our partners such as Sa-Dhan, an apex association of MFIs and other community institutions, realized that a change in the forty-year-old guidelines could reshape the lending ecosystem for household water and toilets. With the launch of SBM two years later, that case became clear to everyone. With the support of MDWS, water and sanitation were officially included within PSL in 2015 – the first such change in its history. The Mission to end open defecation now had the banks on its side.

The other significant enabler has been the proud Indian tradition of self-help groups (SHGs). Both Government and non-Government SHGs have been invaluable to this. Millions of Indian women have come together in SHGs under the National Rural Livelihoods Mission (NRLM), operated by the Ministry of Rural Development, and its state-level counterparts (SRLMs). These women enhance their collective capacity to access finance by taking out group loans from local banks. Through their affiliation with the NRLM, they receive preferential interest rates. And being a group, the women are able to support one another when individual members face the difficulties and vagaries of rural life. From Water.org's perspective, this collective borrowing has been a major factor in the extraordinary rate of repayment we have recorded for our partners' water and sanitation loans, which stands at over 99 per cent in India.

Banks have supported this journey not just by lending to MFIs or by providing credit linkages to SHGs; they have also shown the way by directly lending to households in need and by lending through their business correspondents.

Market-driven Achievements

A repayment rate of over 99 per cent is exceptional for any lending effort at the base of the economic pyramid, on any scale. It is absolutely extraordinary considering that we have catalysed, through our partners, more than 21 lakh loans, in 21 states, to benefit more than 1 crore Indians to date. The finance mobilized? Over Rs 3,000 crore.

More than a third of these borrowers have an income of under Rs 6,500 per month, and two-thirds under Rs 9,000. They are mostly women, majority rural, and they know exactly what they need.

Of the 21 lakh loans, 14 lakh have gone to households wishing to install toilets.

Perhaps this should not be surprising, given the nationwide momentum of SBM and everything we know about the benefits a toilet can bring to a household. But it has been surprising. It has made lenders re-evaluate what it really means to invest in a 'non-productive' asset like a toilet.

Our partners have told us that water and sanitation loans strengthen their overall portfolios, because one of the major reasons for default on other types of loans is illness – and people are healthier and more productive when they can invest in safe water and sanitation. Fewer days are lost to sickness, and fewer hours of the day are lost gathering water and seeking a place to relieve oneself. This is a truth that people know well. It is this truth that has turned SBM into a people's movement like few others the world has seen before.

What Else Is Possible?

India has shown the world how fast a sanitation revolution can happen. It has been unbelievably rewarding to be a part of this revolution, and to help more than 1 crore Indians change their daily lives through access to water and sanitation. India has become a guiding light for other countries confronting basic needs all over the world, including the other countries where Water.org works.

While looking back on the historic success of SBM, we are also in a good position to assess what needs to be done next to sustain an Open Defecation Free future. Water and sanitation credit will play an even more important role post the completion of SBM. It is not sustainable for the Government to continue to provide significant incentives for the creation of water and sanitation infrastructure indefinitely. However, financing will be needed for construction of toilets in new households, refurbishment of toilets that have become dysfunctional, addition of bathing facilities, access to piped water, clean drinking water, etc. Financing will also be needed for budding sanitation entrepreneurs wanting to set up faecal sludge management units, waste collection and treatment businesses and other sanitation enterprises. To plug this funding gap, and ensure the ODF movement is sustained, steady flow of affordable credit is critical.

To achieve this, few measures are necessary:

- Lending under the new PSL guidelines needs to take off exponentially. After the first change in decades, it will take time for credit to flow, banks to develop expertise, guidance to reach all the way to branch offices, and customers to find out. Well-planned incentives and encouragement need to be extended to banks to develop water and sanitation loan products and provide it to customers in need. Similarly, customers need to be made aware of the availability of loans for water and sanitation through mass communication campaigns. With the right enabling factors, the newly sanitation-aware lenders and customers will ensure a sustainable open defecation free India.
- Meanwhile, the self-help groups will continue to play a key role. The NRLM has recently taken a very important step by adding toilet construction to its guidelines as an eligible loan product for SHGs. This recognizes that rural women consider toilet construction to be a fundamental form of self-help, and we couldn't agree more. Since this regulatory change, Water.org has been partnering with SRLMs in Maharashtra and Madhya Pradesh to undertake focused pilots and showcase what these women can really achieve when they apply their savings and shared borrowing power to secure their water and sanitation needs. We now need to scale this effort further, taking it across the nation.

We know that lending to people with limited spending power to meet their water and sanitation needs is a commercially viable and sustainable business proposition. And given the enormous global financing gap, we know it is necessary. This is true in countries with zero public support, but also in countries with very strong public support, like India. It is here, where public commitments, market-driven solutions, and household investments all work together, that our shared goals – be they the Sustainable Development Goal on water and sanitation for all, or the goal of sustaining an open defecation free country – stand within reach, and no gap is too wide to cross. Investment in sanitation pays dividends that can sustain a market and empower lives; and with so many lives changed, it is transforming India.

A Mission Decentralized

AMITABH KANT

Chief Executive Officer, NITI Aayog

The Cost of Poor Sanitation

SANITATION IS A critical determinant of health. Inadequate sanitation especially affects children under the age of five, as their immunity is not yet strong enough to fight off various diseases. Research has shown that long-term malnutrition, as a result of parasites in the child's body, not only prevents necessary physical and cognitive development but also results in stunted physical and cognitive growth. Children who fall ill frequently also miss school often, leading to poor learning outcomes. An ailing child is also likely to spread infections to his or her peers. When girl students reach adolescence, the absence of proper toilets in schools is a problem, and keeps them from attending school while menstruating, causing them to eventually drop out of school. Sanitation alone can thwart many of these effects among children. In addition to the ill-effects on the health and education of young girls and women, the lack of safe sanitation facilities also makes them vulnerable to fear, shame and harassment during open defecation.

A 2006 World Bank study estimated that inadequate sanitation accounted for a loss of $53.8 billion in India, which formed 6.4 per cent of the country's GDP in that particular financial year. The study analyzed the evidence with respect to the adverse economic impacts of inadequate sanitation, including the costs associated with death and disease, accessing and treating water, as well as losses in education, productivity, time and tourism.

How Swachh Bharat Is Different

Under the Swachh Bharat Mission (SBM), sanitation coverage in rural India has increased from 39 per cent in October 2014 to 99.3 per cent as of June 2019. Over 9.7 crore toilets have been constructed in rural India since the Mission began. More than 5.6 lakh villages and 622 rural districts of India have declared themselves Open Defecation Free (ODF). As per the National Annual Rural Sanitation Surveys (NARSS) 2018–19 and 2017–18, the Quality Council of India (QCI) Survey of 2017, as well as the National Sample Survey Office (NSSO) survey of 2015, more than 90 per cent of toilets in the country are being used by household members – this shows a discernible behaviour change in the sanitation habits of rural India.

As we witnessed this grand revolution and the incredible impact it was already making on the ground, some naysayers were bound to surface. A popular misconception among critics in this respect has been that SBM is just another sanitation programme, much like other initiatives that have been implemented by previous governments over the decades. It's always useful to set the record straight.

Firstly, with SBM, the programme has been supported right from the get-go by strong political will and inspiring leadership at the highest levels. The Prime Minister himself is personally championing the cause of a Clean India at multiple national and international fora. In fact, the Mission was launched following a clarion call issued by the Prime Minister to make the country ODF by 2 October 2019,

Mahatma Gandhi's 150th birth anniversary. SBM has always found mention in the Prime Minister's monthly 'Mann Ki Baat' addresses and other public speeches, inspiring the masses to become a part of the sanitation revolution in India. In fact, since his first ever 'Mann Ki Baat' broadcast in 2014, the Mission has figured 37 times in his first 50 addresses! It is his personal commitment towards ensuring the success of the Mission that has further encouraged other senior political leaders including Union Ministers, Chief Ministers, Members of Parliament, Members of the Legislative Assemblies, and even local leaders to spread the message of swachhata in their respective spheres of influence. Consequently, government officials too have put sanitation high on the agenda in their respective Ministries and Departments.

The second aspect of SBM that distinguishes it from other programmes focused primarily on construction of toilets is the Mission's emphasis on behaviour change and its focus on outputs and outcomes. The other schemes mistakenly assumed that the use of a constructed toilet was a given, and progress was reported in all these previous programmes in terms of simply 'toilets built'. SBM is the first sanitation programme in India that has been demand-driven, as opposed to being supply-driven, and has measured success in terms of ODF villages and districts, instead of mere toilet construction.

Decentralized Monitoring and Use of Technology

A relatively lesser-known aspect of the Mission is its unwavering focus on decentralized monitoring through the extensive use of modern technology. Villages declared ODF are verified within three months of declaration by block and district officials. Almost 90 per cent of villages declared ODF have been verified successfully as of the writing of this piece and concurrent verification continues to happen as more and more villages progressively declare themselves ODF. In case any gaps are identified during verification, block officials are informed and asked to take corrective measures in a timely manner, following which another round of verification is done. This process is continued till a village is satisfactorily verified to have become genuinely ODF. Meanwhile, all components of the Mission – construction, payment of incentives, ODF declaration, verification, and even active personnel in every village – are all reported on a real-time basis by states, districts, gram panchayats and villages on the Integrated Management Information System (IMIS) of SBM.

Every toilet constructed under the Mission is mandatorily geotagged so as to ensure that the process is completely transparent. SBM has a special geo-tagging app which is designed exclusively for this purpose and is used widely by swachhagrahis and ground-level officials working in the villages, blocks and districts of India. As I write this, 90 per cent of toilets built under the Mission so far have been geotagged, and this number is rising on a daily basis. Technology is also being used heavily for capacity building at scale through virtual learning and a master trainer ecosystem, so as to sustain the lessons learned and behaviour change effected by the Mission in these five years.

The SBM-Grameen dashboard has become somewhat of a symbol of progress in action, with its ticking clock of toilets that shows the constant and speedy progress the Mission has been making on the ground in real time. This dashboard is connected, at the back end, to IMIS in real-time that is tracking progress on the ground as reported by districts and states concurrently. The IMIS has a plethora of data and information about the programme available on it, and the dashboard merely pulls the highlights out of it. The level of detail to which the IMIS goes, however, in tracking not just the building of toilets but a plethora of factors around it – geo-tagging of toilets, conversion of previous programmes' dysfunctional toilets into functional, community toilets, behaviour change communication, details of swachhagrahis in every village – is a testimony to the commitment of the Mission to absolute transparency.

Aspirational Districts and Other Government Programmes

The Government of India launched the Aspirational Districts programme in January 2018, to improve the socio-economic conditions in 117 backward districts in the country. The programme focuses on five key themes, including access to water and sanitation infrastructure. All themes have a direct bearing on the quality of life and economic productivity of citizens. It is a testimony to the all-pervasive success of SBM that it has been able to deliver equally and successfully in these challenging districts as well. The rural sanitation coverage in these districts is almost at par with the national sanitation coverage, which speaks volumes about the programme's overarching impact across the entire nation.

Even more recently, the Ministry of Women and Child Development launched the POSHAN Abhiyaan, a multi-ministerial convergence mission with the vision to ensure attainment of malnutrition-free India by 2022. Not only is SBM a critical component towards achieving the targets set out by the POSHAN Abhiyaan, it has also inspired the scheme in its strategy for implementation. Along the lines of the cadre of 500 young Zila Swachh Bharat Preraks, who stormed the districts across rural India and supported SBM implementation, a new cadre of Swasth Bharat Preraks has been created to function as catalysts for fast-tracking the implementation of the POSHAN Abhiyaan.

Impact of the Mission

The progress figures are not even the most impressive achievement of the Mission. The true proof of the pudding is in the impact it has already started showing on health, safety, dignity and environmental outcomes.

As per a 2018 World Health Organization report, it is estimated that SBM will have prevented over 3 lakh diarrhoeal deaths by the time India becomes ODF on 2 October 2019 – a milestone not far from us. UNICEF (2017) has estimated that each family in an ODF village in India saves approximately Rs 50,000 per year on decreased medical costs, fewer sick days and the value of lives saved. Similarly, a study conducted by the Bill & Melinda Gates Foundation highlighted that there were 46 per cent fewer cases of diarrhoea among children in villages that had been declared ODF as compared to villages that had not achieved that status. A UNICEF 2019 study also found that ODF villages are 12.7 times less likely to have groundwater contamination traceable to human faecal contamination.

The Way Forward: Sustaining the Progress

Based on the current rate of progress, the entire country will achieve ODF status well before the end of the programme. Unfounded criticism notwithstanding, a question worth asking is: What next? The country has, in the past, experienced the pitfalls of considering sanitation a one-time exercise. Many villages in the country were handed Nirmal Gram Puraskars with great fanfare a few years back. A few years down the line, however, it was found that many households in these villages had slipped back into old habits like open defecation. The country was littered with dysfunctional toilets which the Government had built but the people had not used.

This is because while behaviour can be modified even in a short period of time, evidence suggests that in order to produce a sustained change, behaviour-change campaigns need to be implemented on a regular basis. To safeguard against the possibility of families reverting to old habits, the SBM guidelines incentivize on-ground swachhagrahis to continue their door-to-door messaging, regular verifications and early morning nigrani visits to open-defecation hotspots in the village long after it has been declared ODF.

In order to be effective, behaviour-change communication campaigns need to be tailored to local cultures and contexts. For instance, applying positive peer pressure, creating associations between toilet construction and an aspirational lifestyle, reinforcing the association between shame and open defection on the one hand, and pride and clean toilets on the other, are all strong communication levers used under SBM.

Incentives and benefits need to be designed for promoting the use of infrastructure. For example, a teacher or student who champions the cause of sanitation in school or plays a vital role in maintaining facilities could be rewarded appropriately. The personal habits of children are in the process of being shaped and they can also act as change agents for their communities. Messages pertaining to health and hygiene have been integrated into the school curriculum under SBM.

Going forward, the focus must shift towards encouraging the adoption of basic hygiene practices such as handwashing with soap. It is estimated that handwashing can reduce the incidence of diarrhoea and acute respiratory infections by 40 per cent and 20 per cent respectively. Also, we constantly need to innovate and develop ecologically robust and cost-effective technology options in the sanitation sector that are better suited to local conditions and resource availability. Technologies that have been successfully piloted in different parts of India or in other countries need to be scaled up, following the necessary adaptations.

The quality, pace and scale of progress made under SBM is undeniable and reflected in the ground realities. At the time of its independence, Singapore faced many of the challenges we are grappling with today, including poor sanitation, disease and poverty. Realizing that prevention is far better than cure, national campaigns such as 'Keep Singapore Clean' were launched soon after the country became independent. In a relatively short span of time, the philosophy of cleanliness extended beyond sanitation to various aspects of people's lives, including water, food, cooking practices, the environment, and even corruption.

All told, India has a similar opportunity to make history. SBM has provided a solid foundation. The Government obviously has a big role to play, and so does every citizen of the country, to ensure that we realize Mahatma Gandhi's dream of a Clean India.

PARTNERSHIPS

The Swachh Bharat Mission built several strategic partnerships with Government Ministries, development partners, media and other prominent influencers to ensure the mainstreaming of sanitation in all sectors. These partnerships helped the Mission scale best practices on behaviour change rapidly across the country, as well as accelerate the pace of their adoption.

Swachh Bharat: India Achieves the Unachievable

ARVIND PANAGARIYA

Professor, Columbia University

DURING A BRIEFING session several months prior to the 2014 elections, I had the opportunity to discuss with the then Chief Minister of Gujarat, Narendra Modi, the future course of economic and social policy. When it came to the health sector, I urged the Chief Minister to pay special attention to public health as Prime Minister, should he win the upcoming elections.

I reasoned that over the decades, the Government had concentrated on the provision of medical services, which even the private sector provided. At the same time, it had neglected public health, which only the Government can provide. The result, for instance, was that the drainage systems in our cities had become so badly clogged that even moderate rains resulted in stagnant water bodies that then served as breeding grounds for vector-borne diseases. I went on to add that the old tradition of parents inculcating in their children the habit of washing their hands first thing after entering home and before every meal had also been dying. As Prime Minister, through television broadcasts and other mediums, Modi could exhort parents to instill good personal hygiene habits in children.

The Chief Minister patiently listened and then said: '2 October 2019 will be the 150th birth anniversary of Mahatma Gandhi. Why not resolve to gift the father of the nation a Swachh Bharat on that day!'

I must confess that I did not fully appreciate the significance of what he had said at the time. It was only when I heard him announce, in his maiden address to the nation from the Red Fort on 15 August 2014, the Swachh Bharat Mission (SBM) that I understood the meaning of his words that afternoon in Gandhinagar. In retrospect, it is clear to me that Modi had been thinking about transforming India in all its aspects for a lot longer than any of us may have realized.

Of the numerous schemes, projects, and policy reforms that Modi launched during the last five years, if I were asked to pick just one that will have the greatest long-term impact on the lives of people, it would have to be SBM. Ending open defecation, freeing cities and villages from litter and stagnant water, cleaning up the air we breathe, and bringing clean drinking water to all are essential to the long and healthy lives of citizens. While the current focus of SBM has been on ending open defecation and freeing cities and villages of litter, eventually, providing clean drinking water to all should be a critical component of policy as well.

Unprecedented Success of Swachh Bharat

SBM has made a perceptible difference to the level of cleanliness in Indian cities, with citizens sensitized to the importance of a litter-free environment as never before. But its greatest impact has been ending open defecation in rural areas. On 2 October 2014, the day SBM was officially launched, only 38.7 per cent rural household had toilets. With 9.7 crore additional toilets built, this proportion stood at 99.1 per cent in early May 2019. All states and Union Territories (UTs) except Goa, Odisha and Telangana had achieved 100 per cent sanitation coverage in rural areas by this time.

These are the official figures of the Government of India. It can be plausibly argued that the pressure to show progress leads local officials to exaggerate their achievements. But the National Annual Rural Sanitation Survey (NARSS 2018–19), conducted by an independent verification agency selected via open competition under the World Bank support project to SBM-G, broadly confirms these achievements for rural India. This survey is supervised from beginning to end by an expert working group – co-chaired by Professor Amitabh Kundu, a former member of the National Statistical Commission, and Dr N.C. Saxena, a member of the National Advisory Council chaired by Mrs Sonia Gandhi during the United Progressive Alliance Government. The expert group also includes as members, representatives of the World Bank, UNICEF, WaterAid, BMGF, NSSO, NITI Aayog and the Indian Sanitation Coalition.

Based on a sampling framework that covers 6,136 villages, 92,040 households, 5,782 schools, 5,803 Anganwadi Centres, 1,015 public toilets and 6,055 public spaces, NARSS 2018–19 is among the largest sanitation surveys conducted in India until 2019. The selection of villages and households within them is random and statistically representative in each state, making the sample representative of India. It collected its data between November 2018 and February 2019 and found that, nationwide, 93.1 per cent of households had access to toilets. Of the villages verified as Open Defecation Free (ODF) by the Government, the survey confirmed 90.7 per cent as being so. The survey also found 95.4 per cent of all villages surveyed having minimal litter and stagnant water. A particular concern among critics has been that households with toilets often do not use them. Therefore, NARSS 2018–19 made special effort to collect data on toilet usage. Contrary to popular belief, it found that a whopping 96.5 per cent of the households with access to toilets used them.

The first round of NARSS was carried out in 2017–18. This fact allows us to measure the progress achieved in 2018–19 over that in 2017–18. The proportion of households with access to toilets rose from 77 per cent in 2017–18 to 93.1 per cent in 2018–19. The proportion of households with access to toilets that used toilets rose from 93.4 per cent to 96.5 per cent. But the proportion of villages officially verified as ODF and confirmed to be so fell from 95.6 per cent to 90.7 per cent. This last finding suggests that sustaining collective behavioural change at the level of the village over a long period is a challenge and this is where the Government will need to persist in its efforts.

Notwithstanding its large sample size and supervision by multiple independent experts and agencies, critics have questioned NARSS for its overly optimistic findings. They cite their own surveys to argue that the actual achievements are far more modest. However, these surveys are relatively small and unrepresentative of the country as a whole, and as such cannot serve to make any generalizations of the findings to the nation as a whole. As of now, NARSS remains the most reliable survey. That said, it is important to take the critics seriously wherever outside agencies are conducting scientifically sound surveys without any involvement of the Government.

Even if one disputes the findings of NARSS, there is little scope for doubting the fact that since the launch of SBM, unprecedented progress has been made in ending open defecation in India. Even if the achievements as documented by NARSS are substantially discounted, it can be safely concluded that India is within striking distance of becoming open-defecation free. What had seemed a distant goal five years ago is within India's grasp today. Unsurprisingly, early scepticism that building toilets does not mean much since they go mostly unused, commonly expressed by critics, has all but receded into the background.

The Road Ahead: Three Additional Swachh Bharat Challenges

To be sure, as we enter the year of the 150th birth anniversary of Mahatma Gandhi, we must applaud and celebrate those who helped bring India this close to eliminating open defecation. At the same time, in the midst of the euphoria generated by this success, we can scarcely afford to lose the momentum SBM has generated. Much remains to be done to *sustain* a Swachh Bharat in all its aspects and we must capitalize on the momentum generated by the journey so far to end open defecation.

In particular, perhaps in another ten years, we must aspire to improve our cleanliness standards to globally acceptable levels in three important areas. First, we must further accelerate the movement towards achieving clean cities and villages. This will require behavioural change on at least as large a scale as has been necessary to end open defecation, if not larger. As Indians, we like to clean our immediate surroundings, but only to then drop the waste and litter outside our premises. We must inculcate the habit of collecting waste, separating what can be recycled and then safely disposing the rest using modern methods and technology – local governments have a significant role to play in this enterprise. We also need to make drainage systems in the cities and villages functional so that rains do not create bodies of stagnant water. This is a critical aspect of public health that remains unaddressed.

The second important area that requires attention for the creation of a healthy environment is the air we all breathe. Pollution levels in Indian cities today are many times what any reasonable standard would recommend. This has resulted in a high incidence of breathing problems. For parents bringing up their children in even smaller cities, air pollution is a major cause of worry today. This is an area on which both the Central and state governments must turn their focus as soon as possible.

Finally, we need to ensure the availability of clean water for all. With vast economies of scale in laying down pipelines carrying water, this is a natural monopoly at the local level and calls for provision or coordination by the Government. Over the years, the quality of tap water in India has deteriorated so much that even citizens with limited incomes have had to resort to the costly solution of relying on bottled water. Besides the problem of contamination of piped water where it exists, we also have the problem of lack of availability of any piped water in large parts of the country. In many of these cases, the absence of clean water reservoirs that could serve as the source of piped water adds to the challenge.

The Government has already begun to make efforts in this direction. I am given to understand that piped water supply for all will be implemented in mission mode by making it a people's movement, on similar lines as SBM.

In Conclusion

The challenge of a Clean India that meets the standards observed in developed countries is one we will have to work towards in the years to come. The good news, however, is that the success in ending open defecation in rural India in the last five years offers us hope as well as inspiration for conquering the challenges that remain in the foreseeable future. As India emerges as the third largest economy in the world in the next eight to ten years, it can also emerge as a nation with clean cities, clean air and clean drinking water for all.

Evaluating the Revolution at the Grassroots

ADIL ZAINULBHAI

Chairman, Quality Council of India

IN RESPONSE TO the Prime Minister's push for an Open Defection Free (ODF) India, the largest behaviour change programme in the world was launched in 2014, under the aegis of the Ministry of Drinking Water and Sanitation (MDWS): the Swachh Bharat Mission (SBM). As the movement became stronger, it looked as though India would make significant progress in a short time. In just about five years, access to individual household toilets has increased from nearly 38 per cent in 2014 to 99 per cent in 2019.

But a common question, and sometimes critique, has been – 'Is this really happening on the ground? Are toilets actually being built and then used by people?' In 2016, MDWS asked the Quality Council of India (QCI) to create a system for measuring this in the top 75 districts of India, and then across the country in 2017, in a statistically significant and nationally representative way. The idea on our end was to be 100 per cent efficient and scan every state and district in India within 90 days!

The QCI is an autonomous organization, and its mandate is improving quality in all spheres of life in India. Improving Government services is an important part of the mandate, and

QCI has done several large-scale studies to measure the on-ground progress and impact of Government programmes.

MDWS has developed an online monitoring system for SBM-G, an Integrated Management Information System (IMIS). Household-level data with respect to sanitation facilities of all gram panchayats in the country are fed into the IMIS by states on the basis of the Baseline Survey 2012–13, and updated as need be. Each toilet built is geo-tagged and uploaded through the SBM geo-tagging app to a central database maintained by MDWS.

Likewise, MDWS has an annual third-party monitoring mechanism that tracks the progress of the scheme on a real-time basis which helps in course correction. In addition to QCI, independent verification agencies like the National Sample Survey Organization (NSSO) and National Annual Rural Sanitation Survey (NARSS) have audited the claims mentioned in the IMIS from time to time through on-ground surveys of households, schools, public health centres, and various other community congressional places.

The first such survey to check the access and usage of the toilets was conducted by NSSO in 26 states and Union Territories in 2015 followed by QCI in 2016 and 2017. It is a matter of pride for our organization to have been a part of Swachh Survekshan Grameen 2016 and Swachh Survekshan Grameen 2017.

Swachh Survekshan Grameen 2016 was conducted in the 75 best-performing districts (53 in the Plains and 22 in North Eastern and Special Category) which were identified on the basis of IMIS data available with the Ministry. The household survey covering 70,000 households was carried out in these districts from 21 May 2016 to 20 June 2016. A team of 150 qualified assessors was deployed to collect the required data with the help of a mobile application. The villages were selected based on proper sampling wherein each district was divided into four zones and then villages were randomly chosen from each zone. A minimum of 1,050 households were selected from each district in the Plains and a minimum of 350 households were selected from each district in the North East and Special

Category. Mandi, Himachal Pradesh, and Sindhudurg, Maharashtra, respectively, were the frontrunners in the North East and Special and the Plains categories.

In Swachh Survekshan Grameen 2017, the survey was conducted in 4,626 villages from May to June 2017. The villages were selected based on the Probability Proportional to Size technique, subject to a minimum of 20 villages in each district and 30 households in each village chosen through Simple Random Sampling. A team of 300 qualified assessors was deployed. The study was divided into two categories: Household Survey and Direct Observation. The Household Survey captured parameters like Access to Toilet, Usage of the Toilet and Solid and Liquid Waste Management at the Household Level. Direct Observation collected information regarding access to toilet and cleanliness at common places in a village, i.e. school, anganwadi and public health centre. To validate the sampling methodology, QCI approached experts in the field from various organizations including the NSSO, Indian Statistical Institute, and various universities in India and the USA.

The overall results indicated that rural sanitation coverage had increased from 38.70 per cent in 2014 to 62.45 per cent in May–June 2017, as compared to 63.73 per cent according to the SBM-G IMIS for the same period – a testament to its robustness. The best performing states were Haryana, Kerala, Himachal Pradesh, Manipur, Tripura, Sikkim and Nagaland.

Behaviour change takes time and our surveys made for some interesting findings, beyond access and usage of safe sanitation practices. One common phenomenon was what we now call 'Respondent bias'. Given that it is now common knowledge in rural India that the Government supports economically weaker households with a financial incentive of Rs 12,000 for building and using their toilets, our surveyors found respondents taking that into account during the survey. For instance, in Uttar Pradesh, some households would deny having toilets when our assessors visited them, hoping to become eligible for another round of incentives. This became an operational challenge for us since it affected the sampling across many villages. To overcome such challenges, we went for resampling of the households that were to be visited by an assessor.

Our execution strategy involved 'three levels of defense' to maintain a robust trail of on-ground data, which are as follows:

- A hub-based 'Adaptive training model' was developed in which groups of assessors were trained in 10 locations (Delhi, Mumbai, Kolkata, Bengaluru, etc.) in technical parameters and technological know-how. Following this, they were drilled on the ground using an app-based draft questionnaire.
- Assessors were shortlisted on the basis of their education and professional experience (at least a graduate with a minimum of 2 years of experience in surveying and quality assessments).
- A cloud-based IT platform was developed on which the responses submitted by the assessors using a mobile application were synchronized on a real-time basis. A dedicated 24×7 control room was centralized at the QCI head office to monitor the field assessment on a real-time basis and perform a second-level quality assessment to ascertain the consistency of the survey.
- The surveyed households were called to ensure that the responses were marked correctly by the assessors.
- QCI personnel went as external observers and shadowers to validate the data collected by the assessors on a random basis.

The design parameters were such that we were receiving rapid responses while we were performing a quality check of real-time data. The hit rate of the number of villages went up to 200 per day covering 6,000 households. The operational assessment planning entailed a lot of brainstorming to progressively collect the data and maintain its sanctity at the same time. We initiated a pilot to understand the nitty-gritty of the subject on the ground before expanding the scope of the survey. At some stages, we had to check the geographical spread of responses so that statistically significant conclusions could be drawn from the sample.

One of the challenges that we faced during the assessment was collecting data in difficult terrain where access to public transport was limited. In some villages in Arunachal Pradesh the assessors had to cross fluttering ropeway bridges to carry out the survey! Poor network connectivity in certain parts of the country was another big issue as it made it difficult for the assessors to upload their data in real time. The vagaries of the weather in different parts of the country made our task even more challenging. In Siddipet, Telangana, our assessor fainted in the jungle due to extreme heat. His mobile phone was stolen and we could not establish any contact with him for a few hours. Thankfully some local people took him to a nearby clinic and he recovered there. In another instance, in the Andaman and Nicobar Islands, torrential rainfall made it nearly impossible to conduct the survey. Even after the survey had been conducted, the telecom networks were jammed and the data had to be sent on CDs all the way to Delhi.

Through our survey, we found that 91.29 per cent of the households with access to toilets were also using them regularly, indicating a paradigm shift in the attitude of rural households towards open defecation. One cannot help but admire the sensational change that SBM has brought about even in these remotest of villages.

Of course, there has been criticism from some NGOs and media, often based on anecdotal experiences in a few villages. But the data speaks for itself. The surveys conducted by QCI looked at over 1,40,000 households and are representative of what is happening in every district, and hence a validation of the success of Swachh Bharat to date.

The impact on lives also speaks for itself. The QCI teams found many powerful examples of communities' lives being transformed as a result of the progress made by SBM. In East Sikkim, one of the first districts in the country to be declared ODF, the attendance of girl students in schools improved after separate toilets were constructed for them, and many girls who had previously dropped out returned to their classes. In West Bengal, the unsafe waste disposal from kachcha toilets was causing many health issues. But once pucca toilets were built at homes under SBM, usage went up as there was no longer any foul odour around the toilet. In Arunachal Pradesh, we came across moving stories of people saying that they were 'not compelled to defecate with pigs any more'. Before SBM, households were compelled to defecate in the open which attracted pigs in that area. An elder from the family had to always accompany children when they went to defecate in order to ensure their safety and security. Once safe toilets were constructed under SBM, life became safer for the people, especially kids.

The above is just a taste. Our assessors captured hundreds of such heart-warming stories of how toilets have improved the lives of individuals and families, across communities on video ... but that's for another day, and perhaps another essay.

'The cause of many of our diseases is … our bad habit of disposing of excreta anywhere and everywhere.' – Mahatma Gandhi, *Navajivan Weekly*, May 1925

On 15 August 2014, during his maiden Independence Day address from the ramparts of the Red Fort in New Delhi, Prime Minister Narendra Modi made a clarion call to the nation for an Open Defecation Free India by 2 October 2019.

The Swachh Bharat Mission was launched by the Prime Minister from Rajpath, New Delhi, on 2 October 2014.

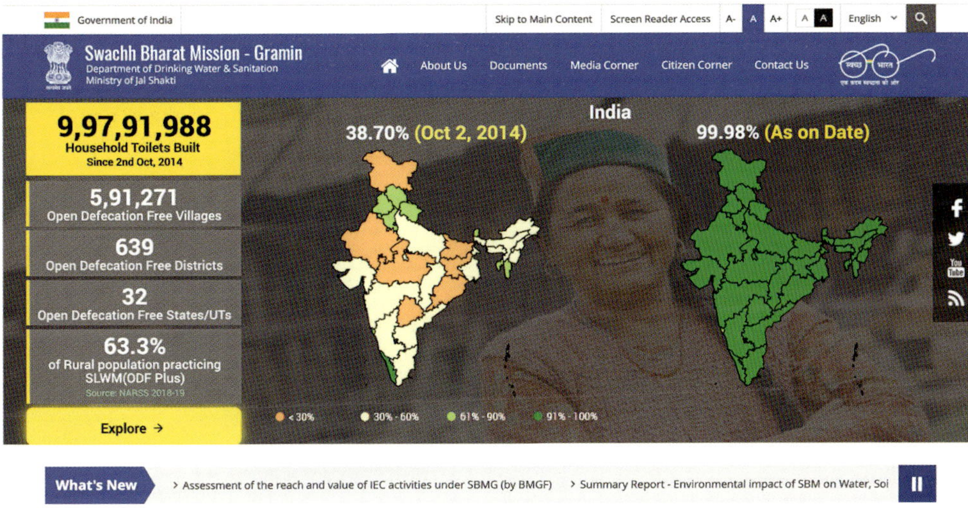

The SBM Integrated Management Information System (IMIS) includes a dashboard that is updated in real time as per reports being uploaded by the states. (Screenshot from August 2019)

Mata Amritanandamayi has made the largest single contribution to the Swachh Bharat Kosh – Rs 100 crore. She was felicitated by the Prime Minister on 2 October 2018 at the Mahatma Gandhi International Sanitation Convention in New Delhi.

Chandrakant Kulkarni, a retired teacher from Pimpri-Chinchwad, Pune, donated 52 post-dated cheques of Rs 5,000, a significant proportion of his pension, to the Swachh Bharat Kosh in June 2016.

Inspired by the Swachh Bharat Mission, 105-year-old Kunwar Bai Yadav of Raipur, Chhattisgarh, sold her goats to raise the money to build a toilet in 2016.

Uttara Thakur, a differently abled young sarpanch from Chhattisgarh, went door-to-door motivating people to use toilets.

Schoolgirl Lavanya (centre) went on a hunger strike in 2016, demanding her parents to build and use a toilet at home. She went on to inspire all 80 households in her village of Halenahalli, Karnataka, to build toilets.

The India Sanitation Conference (Indosan) was inaugurated by the Prime Minister in New Delhi on 30 September 2016 to reiterate the commitment at the highest political level to ensure a Swachh Bharat by 2019.

The Zila Swachh Bharat Prerak programme was launched in New Delhi on 16 December 2016 in collaboration with the Tata Trusts and with an aim to place one young professional in each district across the country to support the district administrations in implementing SBM. Over 500 young professionals were eventually deployed across the country.

The Prime Minister felicitated women swachhata champions at the Swachh Shakti event in Gandhinagar, Gujarat, on the occasion of International Women's Day on 8 March 2017. Over 6,000 women sarpanchs (village heads) and swachhagrahis (village motivators) from all states participated in the event, and attended the grand exhibition showcasing their leadership role in SBM.

The Prime Minister at the Swachh Shakti exhibition showcasing the rural toilet pan and twin-pit toilet technology at Mahatma Mandir in Gandhinagar in 2017.

Around 20,000 women sarpanchs and swachhagrahis from across the country were honoured by the Prime Minister as part of Swachh Shakti 2019 in Kurukshetra, Haryana.

Several influencers, celebrities and senior officers of the Government of India emptied twin-pit toilets to encourage their use in rural India, and to de-stigmatize the emptying of pits by households.

Actor and SBM ambassador Akshay Kumar in Khargone, Madhya Pradesh, in April 2017.

Amitabh Kant, CEO, NITI Aayog, in Firozabad, Uttar Pradesh, in November 2018.

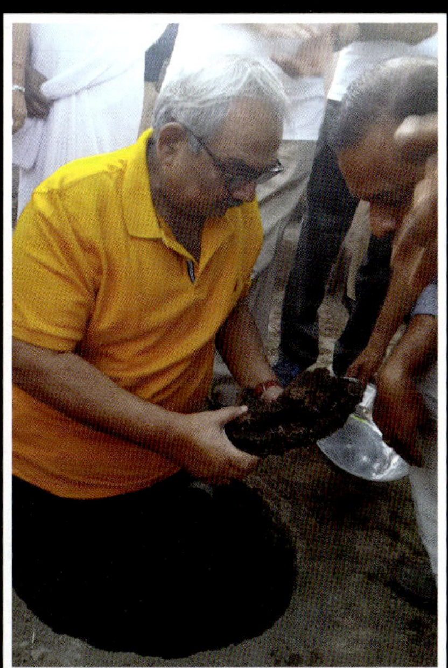

Rajiv Mehrishi, Comptroller and Auditor General of India, in Pune in May 2018.

Parameswaran Iyer, Secretary, Ministry of Drinking Water and Sanitation, in Warangal, Telangana, in February 2017.

The Prime Minister offered shramdaan to construct a toilet in Shahanshahpur village in Varanasi, Uttar Pradesh, on 23 September 2017.

Starting from Jharkhand's Simdega district, women have been trained as head masons (rani mistris) to empower them and to meet the increasing demand for toilets.

Swachhata Hi Seva has been celebrated as a people's campaign every year since 2017, with millions participating in a fortnight-long swachhata drive.

Over 10 crore people participated in Swachhata Hi Seva 2017, and 2.8 crore essays and 2.9 crore paintings were received from schoolchildren.

To launch Swachhata Hi Seva 2018, the Prime Minister interacted with SBM ambassadors, influencers and citizens' groups across 17 locations to re-emphasize and continue the jan andolan for sanitation. The campaign mobilized participation by 20 crore people.

A number of celebrities have come out in support of SBM, undertaking shramdaan or volunteer work to generate awareness about the programme.

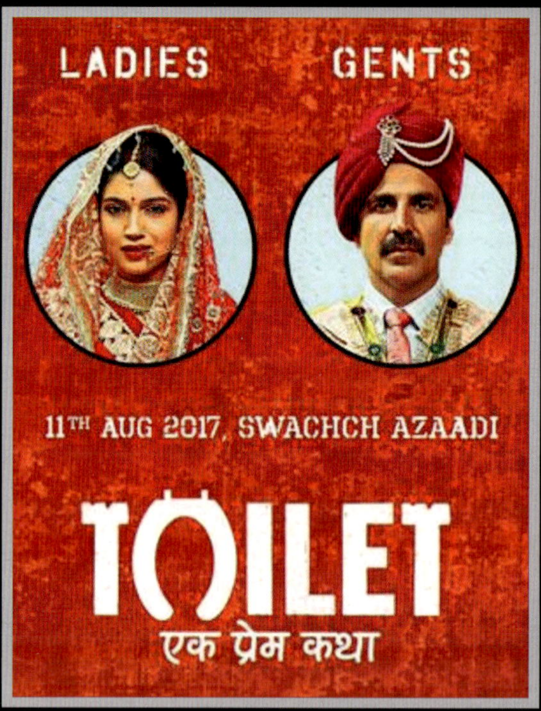

Actors Akshay Kumar and Bhumi Pednekar took sanitation to the silver screen with the film *Toilet – Ek Prem Katha* (Toilet – A Love Story).

Actor Anushka Sharma lent her support to the cleaning of Versova beach in Mumbai during Swachhata Hi Seva in September 2017.

Actor Amitabh Bachchan has been an ambassador for SBM since its inception and has supported the Mission for various campaigns and initiatives, including SBM's iconic '*Darwaza Band toh Bimaari Band*' campaign.

Swachhathon, the first ever Swachh Bharat Hackathon, crowd-sourced innovative and technology-driven solutions to key sanitation challenges from hundreds of budding entrepreneurs from around the world.

SBM started a multi-stakeholder initiative called Swachh Iconic Places (SIP), focusing on the clean-up of 100 places across India that are 'iconic' due to their cultural significance.

Swachhagrahis are the foot soldiers of SBM. Over the past 5 years, a cadre of over 6,25,000 swachhagrahis has triggered lakhs of villages into becoming ODF.

जय माँ शेरावाली

In April 2018, 10,000 swachhagrahis from different parts of the country travelled to Bihar to work with 10,000 local swachhagrahis to 'trigger' behaviour change throughout the state as part of the Chalo Champaran campaign.

The Prime Minister addressing the 20,000 swachhagrahis who participated in the campaign, at Motihari, Champaran, on its culmination on 10 April 2018.

A Swachh Sundar Shauchalaya (decorate your toilet) contest was launched in January 2019 to mobilize rural households to increase ownership and promote the sustained use of toilets, as well as instil a sense of pride among the owners.

ସ୍ୱଚ୍ଛ ଭାରତ
ଆମ ସଭିଙ୍କ ମନର
ବିକଳ୍ପ ,
ସ୍ୱଚ୍ଛ ଭାରତ ଗଢ଼ିବାରେ
କରିବା ସଂକଳ୍ପ ।

B.M) Drass 2017-2018
SWACHH BHARAT
ABHIYAN
WASH YOUR HANDS AFTER THE TOILET
स्वच्छ भारत
स्वच्छ भारत

ಗ್ರಾಮ ಪಂಚಾಯತ್ ಆಲೂರು

The Swachh Survekshan Grameen is a nationwide survey to rank all districts of India on swachhata. This survey has acted as a trigger for villages to re-intensify the jan andolan.

The Mahatma Gandhi International Sanitation Convention, organized in New Delhi from 29 September to 2 October 2018, brought together 55 sanitation ministers and 200 representatives from 70 countries to discuss key issues related to the achievement of sustainable sanitation at scale.

The Swachh Bharat tableau at the Republic Day Parade on 26 January 2019 attempted to depict how Mahatma Gandhi's dream of a Swachh Bharat was the key guiding principle for the SBM.

The theme for the Kumbh Mela in 2019 was Swachh Kumbh, with over 1 lakh toilets installed for the incoming pilgrims. During a special event – Swachh Kumbh, Swachh Aabhar – in Prayagraj, Uttar Pradesh, in February, the Prime Minister felicitated sanitation workers at the Kumbh and washed the feet of five of them to express the nation's gratitude for their service.

A Jan Andolan

AKSHAY ROUT

OSD, Department of Drinking Water and Sanitation, Ministry of Jal Shakti, Government of India

> *'Friends, the way the Swachh Bharat Mission reached every nook and corner of the country in the form of a jan andolan is a case study for many prestigious universities across the world. I think that in the 21st century, this kind of movement for behavioural change has not happened in any other country until now. India is certainly changing. Behaviours and habits are changing.'*
>
> —Prime Minister Narendra Modi, Motihari, 10 April 2018

INHERENT IN THE Prime Minister's words above is the underlying philosophy of India's Swachh Bharat Mission (SBM): the bold but sincere effort to change sanitation behaviours across the country within just 5 years. These deep-seated and socially accepted but unhealthy behaviours – especially open defecation (OD) – have been prevalent among many parts of the population over generations. This was, therefore, a significant challenge for sanitation practitioners in 2014. Neuroscientists agree that it is much easier to adopt 'new' habits than replace old ones that refuse to die.

In the heterogenous context of India, mindsets vary across communities. To some, it was impure to have a toilet in the premises of their homes, to others going out for open defecation was a social outing. For some, toilets were for occasional use when it was raining outside, and for others, toilets were only for women or old people – it was macho to go out. There were also certain areas where topographical challenges made the construction of toilets difficult, and made the task of behaviour change even more arduous. But one thing was clear: the brick and sand and the pan were nominal factors; one had to work primarily on the mind. The key challenge before the Swachh Bharat Mission was to construct a toilet in people's minds, that would then automatically manifest itself on the ground.

The 4 Challenges

The 4Ss – Speed, Scale, Stigma and Sustainability – were major tasks to deal with. In 2014, the harsh reality that awaited the Mission was that there were no enthusiastic takers for the financial incentive and technology support that they brought as supply – unlike the attraction of a house, a gas cylinder, an electric connection, drinking water or even a village road. The foremost task for Information, Education and Communication (IEC) managers then was to create a wave of demand in quick time so that sanitation coverage could jumpstart from the meagre base of 39 per cent. To debunk the various myths and stigmas associated with using toilets, the Swachh Bharat Mission Grameen (SBM-G) undertook a set of interventions, where the message was the real hero.

Unparalleled Leadership: The Communicator-in-Chief

Leading the IEC campaign from the front has been the Prime Minister of India himself. When he spoke from the ramparts of the Red Fort about the urgent need for a Clean India, he brought the taboo topic of 'toilets' and 'open defecation' out of the closet and triggered a thought in the collective consciousness of the nation. Over the last five years, he has proactively taken up every opportunity to send across the message of safe sanitation and achieving an Open Defecation

Free (ODF) India by October 2019. From laying the brick for toilet construction, talking about 'swachhata' in three-fourths of all his 'Mann ki Baat' addresses to the nation, personally presiding over large mass mobilization campaigns, exhorting every organization and every group to take up sanitation activity, felicitating little-known swachhata champions from remote parts, washing the feet of sanitation workers at the Kumbh Mela to taking the agenda to international dialogues, and even highlighting it extensively during his election campaign, the Prime Minister has not lifted his foot off the sanitation pedal even once. He has, in fact, been the Communicator-in-Chief of the Mission, inspiring the country to make the shift from OD to ODF. The Prime Minister's communications have been the most strategic asset of the Mission.

Torchbearers of the Swachh Bharat Mission

At the other end of the spectrum have been the swachhagrahis – 6,25,000 (an average of one in every village of India) foot soldiers of SBM. Swachhagrahis are local volunteers who are trained in raising awareness, triggering and motivation techniques, and are key to changing the mindset around sanitation in their villages. Since they belong to the local community and are aided by local knowledge, language, art and culture, swachhagrahis tailor their interventions to the local context, thereby maximizing their effectiveness. These interventions, based on inter-personal communication (IPC), promote an intense face-to-face dialogue with the community and form the bedrock of all IEC under SBM-G. In the context of a segmented and diverse population, the SBM-G guidelines recognize this and suggest spending 60 per cent of IEC budgets on IPC. While the guidelines provide an indicative list of IPC interventions, the swachhata champions across the country have used their creativity to bring in clutter-breaking, innovative ways of spreading their messages of swachhata, often calling out the pride and honour of the community.

Changing the Sanitation Discourse

SBM-G has undertaken some of the most iconic social mobilization campaigns India has ever seen: Swachhata Hi Seva, Satyagraha Se Swachhagraha, Swachh Sundar Shauchalaya, Swachh Sankalp Se Swachh Siddhi being some of them. The focus has been on promoting safe toilet technologies and inspiring pride in construction and use of toilets for the health and dignity of families. Raising awareness and promoting 'shramdaan' have been the key tenets of these campaigns, along with the push towards achieving SBM-G performance indicators. Taking this opportunity, the top leadership of the country has led from the front, setting an example by offering shramdaan.

Celebrities, faith leaders, social groups, women and children have all come together to turn these campaigns into mass movements. Millions of people (1.34 crore toilets painted during Swachh Sundar Shauchalaya, 2.4 crore essays written during Swachh Sankalp Se Swachh Siddhi, among others) joined these campaigns to make Swachh Bharat a true jan andolan. The Satyagraha Se Swachhagraha Campaign with the rallying cry of 'Chalo Champaran' saw 10,000 swachhagrahis from Bihar and 10,000 swachhagrahis from other states across India uniquely paired together to trigger behaviour change in villages across Bihar. People's participation has, thus, emerged as the top answer to the decades of sanitation backlog. A billion-plus people have wielded the baton and are running tirelessly as one nation to usher in a Swachh India.

Becoming the Voice of a Jan Andolan

Mass media approaches through print and electronic media have left a lasting impression on citizen consciousness. On one hand, there were audio visual campaigns like Darwaza Band featuring Bollywood megastar Amitabh Bachchan and the twin-pit toilet campaign featuring superstar Akshay Kumar; on the other, dozens of opinion articles published in prominent newspapers by the who's who of India have served as significant advocacy. As a part of its mass media outreach, the Mission's central social media handles have provided real-time updates about its priorities and the activities taking place on the ground, as well as its impact.

SBM brand ambassadors like Amitabh Bachchan, Akshay Kumar or Sachin Tendulkar have not been the typical ambassadors hired for an ad campaign, but more of partners at work for the Mission. They joined events and consultations, interacted with the public through discussions on swachhata over social media, honoured champions and engaged in shramdaan. They immersed themselves in the Mission and became stakeholders in its outcome. Swachh Bharat diehard Akshay Kumar even created the Bollywood blockbuster *Toilet: Ek Prem Katha* that certainly is a milestone in sanitation messaging or any civic messaging for that matter. Many such creative pursuits on the once unmentionable subject of sanitation have been taken up on both celluloid and the small screen, including shows like *Chalo Saaf Karein*, *Hum Saaf Saaf Hain*, *Safar Manzilon Ka* and *Main Kuch Bhi Kar Sakti Hoon*. Besides celebrities, politicians and senior administrators too regularly undertake myth-defying demonstrations involving emptying pits, cleaning toilets, digging pits – essentially getting their hands 'dirty' to spread the message of swachhata. Such 'leading by example' IEC interventions were organized to reassure the community and address any dissonance through high-pitched positive noises. The net result is that the chatter is on – in the drawing room, during morning walks, at the village chaupal, in class rooms, at conferences, at tea stalls – about Swachh Bharat, the toilet revolution, overall cleanliness – and it is chatter that is not likely to stop. Everyone has a suggestion, everyone has a complaint, but the talk starts and ends with a note of appreciation about a job well begun and largely well done.

Numbers Don't Lie

Outreach at scale in a country of India's size requires significant finances besides other support systems. *Putting the money where the mouth is,* the SBM-G guidelines provided up to 8 per cent of the programme expenditure for IEC activities, which meant a kitty of close to Rs 6,500 crore over the last four-plus years. A recent study by the Bill & Melinda Gates Foundation (BMGF) further estimates that SBM was able to mobilize an equivalent of Rs 22,000 crore to Rs 28,000 crore from non-SBM stakeholders, in spending for sanitation awareness and behaviour change activities across rural India. The study also estimates that every rural Indian was exposed to SBM-G related IEC messaging about 2,500-3,300 times in the last four years! A case in point is how the Swachh Bharat Mission logo today features on Indian currency notes, the Indian Railways' network and has come to be seen as a ubiquitous and enduring symbol of this country's collective commitment to a Clean India.

Sustaining the Global Dream, Now India's Reality

The Swachh Bharat IEC journey is a national heritage, and indeed a global asset. This is a model that can be adopted by organizations and countries, which need to create mass involvement to realize civic goals with speed and effect. Seventy countries listened to India's sanitation journey with rapt attention at the Mahatma Gandhi International Sanitation Convention (MGISC) in New Delhi in October 2018, a journey that is perhaps the world's greatest story of behaviour change. This unparalleled IEC tale is set to ignite the global community that is tasked with the time-bound Sustainable Development Goal 6.2: ensuring sanitation for all by 2030 – a goal that India is poised to achieve 11 years ahead of schedule.

Mobilizing the Corporate Sector

NAINA LAL KIDWAI

Chair, India Sanitation Coalition

THE CURRENT SWACHH Bharat Mission (Grameen) (SBM-G) has achieved excellent results ever since its launch in October 2014. The nation is swiftly and confidently heading towards Open Defecation Free (ODF) status with over 9.7 crore household toilets having been constructed over a four-and-a-half-year period in rural India, and more than 5,60,000 villages becoming open defecation free. As the programme moves into the next phase, there are policies and plans being put in place, including Faecal Sludge and Septage Management (FSSM), and Menstrual Hygiene Management and Equity, in fulfilling the requirements of attaining Sustainable Development Goals (SDGs) 6, 11 and 17.

This is a matter of satisfaction for all of us who have conceived of and run the India Sanitation Coalition (ISC) with the support of Federation of Indian Chambers of Commerce and Industry (FICCI), the Bill & Melinda Gates Foundation and several corporates, NGOs and development agencies in alignment with the Government's sanitation programme. We have focused on increased participation of the private sector to achieve an ODF and Clean India, documenting and communicating best practices so others can replicate the success and scale up efforts.

Historically, the onus of providing solutions for societal problems, including those of sanitation, has been seen as the Government's responsibility. However, recently, to provide the necessary impetus and additional resources, the non-Government sector has evolved which also brings in the much-needed accountability of public spending. The profit-driven private sector has traditionally been viewed with suspicion. Their efforts are often focused in and around their plants and factories, creating co-benefits and shared value which benefit the company by creating goodwill while accruing benefits to society. Manpower and resources are usually drawn from these villages thus providing employment. Establishing a healthy and disease-free environment helps all in the area – a clear win-win scenario. In addition to leveraging business resources to create social value, corporate social responsibility (CSR) funds provide the opportunity to unlock newer areas of collaboration with the local government and institutions.

ISC has attempted through its efforts to encourage corporates to include sanitation in their CSR spend, which was not their focus earlier. ISC believes in BUMT – Build, Use, Maintain, Treat. We have attempted to identify newer and innovative areas of collaboration where the private sector may play an effective role in enabling access to and use of sanitation services by the population based on the following:

- Working with the private sector to raise demand through sanitation marketing and financing options including access to household credit, financing for local entrepreneurs or via other means;
- Encouraging, enabling and supporting the private sector to meet demand at the household level (product delivery, toilet construction, cleaning services, etc.);
- Fostering the role of the local private sector further along the sanitation chain in transport, disposal and reuse to responsibly manage waste.

There are scores of interventions accommodating one or more of the above which ISC has been seeking to recognize and reward over the last three years and these come alive through the annual ISC-FICCI Sanitation Awards and India Sanitation Conclave.

The ISC-FICCI Sanitation Awards are a conscious and deliberate effort to recognize and reward excellence in the sector, in multiple categories, not only in terms of sanitation spending and entrepreneurship but also in transformation of lives due to the accrued benefits of improved sanitation. Corporates, entrepreneurs, social enterprises, financial institutions, the Government and the media were nominated for these awards and an expert jury, chaired by Padma Vibhushan Dr R.A. Mashelkar, helped to decide the winners.

Among 2019's ISC awardees, the winner in the Best Corporate Initiative category was ITC Limited which, through its Mission Sunehra Kal, implemented Sanitation and Solid Waste Management (SWM) interventions which aligned to the Swachh Bharat Mission and SDG 6. ITC focused both on providing access and driving usage of toilets through behaviour change, in its three-pronged approach to sanitation through individual household toilets and community toilet construction and a WASH-in-School programme. The aim was to promote a hygienic environment in its catchments through prevention of open defecation and reduction in water-borne diseases. It was a community-driven-managed-owned intervention with stakeholders comprising of community members, ward members, Government officials and NGO partners. Community-based organizations such as a WATSAN (Water Sanitation) committee, school management committee, child cabinets and women self-help groups were formed and strengthened for ownership and sustainability. Information, education and communication activities were undertaken to drive behaviour change. Operational in 26 districts across 16 states, a whopping 33,950 household toilets and 44 community toilets were constructed till December 2018. Cumulatively, 1.71 lakh children were found to have benefitted directly from school WASH interventions and 95 per cent of project villages and wards were declared ODF. The proportion of the households that were found to have been using the created infrastructure was more than 95 per cent.

Another awardee in the corporate category (small) was Genrobotics, which was were typically identified with innovations that specialized in design and development of robotic solutions seamlessly integrated with artificial intelligence to address the most pressing social issues. The company, which was founded in 2017 by a young group of passionate engineers, created social impact through the conception, designing and development of 'Bandicoot', a robotic device with a human-controlled interface to clean manholes. Mission Robohole ended up catering to the requirements of SDGs 1, 3, 6, 8, 9, 10, 11 and 17.

Tide Technocrats, awarded in the corporate category (medium-size companies), provides environmental and sustainability solutions in the areas of sanitation, solid waste management, and renewable energy. It is an empanelled organization for SBM by the Ministry of Housing and Urban Affairs, Government of India; a partner organization to the Sustainable Sanitation Alliance (SuSanA); and a member of the National Faecal Sludge and Septage Management (NFSSM) alliance, funded by the Bill & Melinda Gates Foundation in India. They have supported over 170 towns and cities in India, Asia and Africa, helping them achieve their environmental impact. Since 2014, they have been working on developing a solution for sanitation treatment of non-sewered towns and cities. In partnership with other organizations, Tide Technocrats has been able to set up three plants on the ground in Warangal (15KLD), Narsapur (15KLD) and Wai (70KLD) to showcase the biosafe treatment of human waste that is de-sludged from septic tanks. Their contribution was recognized by the ISC-FICCI Sanitation Awards jury as a model showcasing partnerships as a key solution to achieving sustainable solid and liquid waste management.

'Best Engagement Model in Sanitation by a Social Enterprise' is an interesting category in the ISC-FICCI Sanitation Awards with worthy nominations each year. Eram Scientific's 'eToilet', an indigenous and innovative product, won the accolade. It is India's first automatic, unmanned, electronic public toilet. Through this unique product, the company has attempted to address the inherent challenges of unhygienic public sanitation on the whole. The eToilet is 100 per cent environment friendly and developed on a holistic convergence of the latest technologies available in electrical, mechanical, web and mobile spaces. As a result, the eToilet attempts to address existing challenges of sustainable public sanitation in a cost-effective manner. Above all, the firm offers a comprehensive maintenance support mechanism to ensure the sustainable operation of eToilets beyond the commissioning stage. A pan-Indian Service Network of the firm caters to the operation and maintenance of units on the basis of an annual maintenance contract.

The eToilet works on sustainable revenue models of user-fee collection and revenue generated through advertisements. This amount collected can be used for further maintenance and cleaning of the units. There are multiple revenue models, including outright purchase by local bodies, a sponsored model involving CSR funding by corporates, and an entrepreneurship model where the operator can have a parallel revenue stream by getting advertisements on the exterior and walls that accommodate scrolling and back-lit displays.

Another area where ISC has made good headway is WASH financing. A crucial aspect in the sector is the need for large-scale financing in WASH over a range of interventions: households in need of water connections; those left outside the baseline surveys; households that have dysfunctional toilets that require repair now or in the future; and enterprises that work in the sanitation supply chain or solid and liquid waste management. According to a recent analysis undertaken at the behest of the Government, current lending in the sanitation space is less than Rs 700 crore whereas the potential is nearly Rs 80,000 crore. Therefore, sustainable financing streams in WASH buoyed by conducive Government policy and initiatives to promote WASH financing could be a game changer. So, to this end, the CSR Act of 2013 needs to evolve and indeed adapt to the changed India which promises to stay ODF. The ISC is in discussion with the designated High-Level Committee on Corporate Social Responsibility at the Union Ministry of Corporate Affairs for amending existing CSR guidelines to allow CSR funds to be mobilized for innovative funding mechanisms which can further spur India's sanitation movement. Key inclusions would be the use of CSR funds for sanitation credit enhancements and social impact bonds, which have been effectively used in countries the world over. We would also like the CSR Act to allow for CSR funds to be utilized by companies instituting the monitoring mechanism for the comprehensive assessment of WASH compliance by its workers and neighbouring communities and grant monetary rewards to individual worker households within the demographic for 100 per cent WASH compliance in the form of a Swachhata Bonus. In addition to this, ISC is engaging with financial institutions including banks to encourage them to enhance WASH financing permitted under Priority Sector Lending.

Finally, everyone who is involved in SBM realizes that it is crucial to have effective partnerships between stakeholders at all levels – Government Ministries, Departments and agencies responsible for SBM at multiple levels, including local, national and state-level municipalities, regulators and public utilities. Private sector organizations, development partners including bilateral and multilateral donors, CSOs, national and international NGOs, CBOs, networks and alliances, and advocacy and campaigning organizations providing the much-needed impetus that the programme demands from time to time to become a citizens' movement.

As I put forward in my book *Survive or Sink*, I believe that we are on the right path and at a very important inflexion point which will determine the India we want to build.

Sanitation Warriors: The Zila Swachh Bharat Prerak Programme

RATAN N. TATA

Chairman, Tata Trusts

FOR OVER 125 years, Tata Trusts has been at the frontiers of development in India through its approach to philanthropy which aims to bring about a lasting difference in the lives of our communities. Over this period, Tata Trusts has engaged with individuals and Government bodies, international agencies and like-minded organizations to build and nurture a self-sustaining ecosystem working across sectors from water and sanitation, healthcare, nutrition, education and livelihoods to arts, craft, and culture.

Before the Prime Minister, Shri Narendra Modi, announced the Swachh Bharat Mission (SBM) on Independence Day in 2014 from the ramparts of the Red Fort, India ranked among the countries with the worst under-nutrition, stunting and wasting levels in the world, even worse than some countries in sub-Saharan Africa. It had been estimated by various research groups that about 40 per cent of our children were stunted. India contributed to more than half of the world's open defecation, the biggest impediment for the world to achieve clean water and sanitation for all people, which is among the Sustainable Development Goals (SDGs) adopted by the UN in 2015 to be achieved by 2030. Poor levels of sanitation in rural areas have inhibited the effectiveness of nutrition initiatives like the Integrated Child Development Services (ICDS) and the mid-day meal scheme. Lack of sanitation in schools has resulted in a disproportional dropout rate among adolescent girls, many of whom are then married early, have very early pregnancies and children with low birth weight, who are highly susceptible to being malnourished. Stunted and wasted children do not achieve their full physical and cognitive potential, and this hampers their economic potential and their ability to provide better opportunities for their own children. This vicious cycle had to be eliminated.

Through the Tata Water Mission (TWM), the Tata Trusts is committed to provide access to safe drinking water and sanitation, which are both closely linked to nutrition. The Tata Trusts has been not only using the traditional strengths of community mobilization and capacity building, but also the power of innovative approaches and technological solutions. The landmark announcement of 2014 and the expression of political will in solving India's sanitation crisis by none less than the Prime Minister inspired the Trusts to offer its full and unconditional support to the Mission.

The association began with supporting the office of the Secretary, Ministry of Drinking Water and Sanitation (MDWS), with young managerial talent to infuse energy and fresh thinking on the policy front for the Mission. It eventually developed into one of the largest collaborative initiatives supported by the Tata Trusts – the Zila Swachh Bharat Prerak (ZSBP) programme – placing some of the brightest and most highly qualified youth with the district administrations to bring energy and fresh thinking into the implementation of the Mission as well.

The vision for the ZSBP programme too was inspired by the Prime Minister's 'Mann Ki Baat' address on 25 September 2016, during which he appealed to the corporate world to come up with a model whereby young professionals can dedicatedly work at the grass-roots level to ensure the success of SBM-Grameen (SBM-G). In view of this, the Trusts along with the MDWS designed a fellowship programme with the aim to create a cadre of skilled young professionals, who would work with state governments and district administrations to oversee the implementation and monitoring of SBM-G. Through this initiative, Tata Trusts tried to channelize the energy of social capital towards the development of the country.

The young professionals were given the title of Zila Swachh Bharat Prerak and were trained by experts from the MDWS, and the Tata Centre for Development at the University of Chicago, along with the International Innovation Corps in areas of Project Management, Community Approaches to Sanitation and Data-Driven Decision Making. This equipped them to take on the on-ground challenges. The first batch of ZSBPs was deployed in April 2017. Over the next six months, more than 515 ZSBPs were deployed across the length and breadth of the country.

Jamsetji Tata said that a nation or a community advances when we lift up the best and the most gifted so as to make them the greatest service to the country. The ZSBP programme has been a realization of this vision. These young and highly skilled professionals were a diverse lot with backgrounds in management, engineering, law, social work, architecture, medicine. But each one went to the field with the same goal of ensuring that every Indian has access to safe sanitation facilities.

As the ZSBPs began their journey, they soon realized that every state and every district brought with it a unique set of challenges and opportunities. While some dealt with sub-zero temperatures in the hills of Kashmir where conventional toilets did not work as the water in the toilet pan froze and people used unsanitary dry-latrines, others worked in the remote districts of Arunachal Pradesh with scattered habitation and vast tracts of open land where transportation of bricks and cement was an expensive affair due to the absence of motorable roads. But the ZSBPs were unfazed by the challenges and took them in their stride. While some invoked Kashmiri culture and heritage to convince people to build and use sanitary toilets, others pushed the idea of pre-fabricated toilets that suited Arunachal Pradesh's conditions. The ZSBPs had to work around socio-cultural norms, language barriers, lack of resources and, in some cases, even general apathy. But over the past two years, each such challenge has become a success story.

The programme gave a broad job-role to the ZSBPs and left it to the district and state administrations to utilize the assets on-hand. While some ZSBPs worked as Master Trainers, imparting Community-Led Total Sanitation (CLTS) and Community Approaches to Sanitation (CAS) training to ground-level staffs and swachhagrahis, others worked with the administration in finding bottlenecks through data and trend analysis. For example, the ZSBP who joined the programme as the state coordinator in Bihar quickly realized that one of the major stumbling blocks in the state's progress in SBM-G was the gaps in the baseline data. After taking the state and district administrations into confidence, the team under him in Bihar started a baseline validation exercise which led to the identification and removal of some duplicate and some non-existent baseline entries, resulting in instantaneous increase in Individual Household Latrine (IHHL) coverage in Bihar. This illustrates the major driving force ZSBPs have been in the success of SBM-G, and the MDWS has even acknowledged it in various forums.

When the ZSBP programme started in April 2017, the national sanitation coverage stood at 64.46 per cent. The rise in sanitation coverage from 38.7 per cent in 2014 to over 64 per cent was an appreciable increase, but with just over two years remaining to achieve 100 per cent coverage, a major fillip was required. The ZSBP programme was that fillip. As of June 2019, the national coverage stands at 99.05 per cent with over 5.62 lakh Open Defecation Free (ODF) villages. While the credit for this significant improvement goes to all the people associated with SBM-G, the ZSBPs have proven to be a great ally of the district and state administrations wherever they have worked. The ZSBPs have not only played a critical role in ensuring increase in IHHL coverage, but even more importantly, they have ensured substantial improvement in transparency factors like geo-tagging, verification of ODF villages and repair of dysfunctional toilets across the country.

Now, as SBM-G moves towards ODF-plus with focus on ODF Sustainability and Solid and Liquid Waste Management, the ZSBP programme has also stepped into Phase-2 with major focus on innovative ODF Sustainability measures and Waste Management solutions.

The ZSBP initiative was a first-of-its-kind partnership between a philanthropic organization and the Government of India to effect change at such a large scale. The success of Phase-1 of the initiative has certainly brought a remarkable transformation in the sanitation landscape of the country, and is due to all the young professionals who joined in this noble cause and contributed towards this nation-building exercise. For Tata Trusts, the success of the initiative is a testimony to our unwavering commitment to bringing about a lasting difference in the lives of our communities.

Youth in the System

MAHIMA VASHISHT, VINEET JAIN AND KARISHMA KADYAN

Secretary's Office, Department of Drinking Water and Sanitation, Ministry of Jal Shakti, Government of India

'The youth of a nation are the trustees of posterity.'

– Benjamin Disraeli

DISRAELI WAS RIGHT. Major transformation calls for strong agents of change, and the youth of a nation have the potential to become those agents. The Swachh Bharat Mission (SBM) has been no different. The youth in the system have played a significant part in making SBM-Grameen (SBM-G) the jan andolan it is today. Young girls and boys not only demanded safe sanitation facilities for themselves in the villages and districts of rural India, but led the sanitation movement at all levels – convincing their peers and elders to build and use toilets, manage their solid and liquid resources properly, and create a clean and green environment for a better future.

We have all heard incredible stories from the ground these past five years – of young women refusing to marry into houses which do not have a toilet, of youth organizations like the National Cadet Corps and the Nehru Yuva Kendra Sangathan leading the charge in making villages on the banks of the Ganga Open Defecation Free (ODF), of over 4 lakh youth who registered for the Swachh Bharat

Summer Internship in 2018, and of over 500 of India's brightest young professionals who left cushy private-sector opportunities to take on the challenge of making districts ODF as Zila Swachh Bharat Preraks. Meanwhile, at the engine room of the Mission, the office of the Secretary, Ministry of Drinking Water and Sanitation (MDWS), the three of us got the opportunity of a lifetime – to play a part in driving what is undoubtedly the world's biggest behaviour change movement.

Our first interaction with Mr Parameswaran Iyer (who we know now as 'Boss'), Secretary, MDWS, is etched in our minds with indelible ink. We were all bowled over by his 'un-government-like' style of functioning. There was no time wasted on formalities, and the conversation was honest. He was clear about the role he saw us playing in the system: bring in energy, creativity, agility and disruption to the Mission. He made no bones about the challenges he saw us facing, and was forthright about where we could expect support from the system and where we would be on our own.

The job was unique – it came with no fixed job description, though over the next few months, we each found our niche based on our interests and strengths.

It was challenging; we were outsiders in a system, functioning like insiders. It was uncharted territory – none of us came with any background in sanitation – and it was all the more exciting for being so. Most of all though, it was an incredible opportunity – if we succeeded, we would be playing a significant role in the team working on one of the largest behaviour change efforts ever attempted, and the biggest social revolution rural India has ever seen.

When two of us joined the Ministry from our parent organization, Tata Trusts, the brief given to us was that we were to offer executive support to the Secretary 'for a few weeks'. As we write this, we have now spent over three years in this job, and cut three anniversary cakes a few days after Boss each year. The third of us, who began her association with the Mission as a Zila Swachh Bharat Prerak (ZSBP), has also cut her first anniversary cake.

Infusing 'Youthful Energy and Innovation' into the System

Boss is (in)famous in the Water, Sanitation and Hygiene (WASH) circles for his unbelievable energy levels, and for good reason. He leads by example and his personal enthusiasm laid the foundation for our first task at the Ministry – bringing energy into the system.

This boost of energy was not to be limited to the Secretary's office. A few months into the stint, when we all realized that the model of bringing 'youth into the system' was working well, it seemed natural to extend the model beyond the Ministry. Thus was born the Zila Swachh Bharat Prerak programme. The Prime Minister issued a clarion call during one of his 'Mann Ki Baat' addresses to corporates to support the Mission by sending young professionals to aid the district collectors in replicating the success of the model countrywide. Soon after, the Tata Trusts came forward with the offer to build a cadre of close to 600 young professionals who were placed in the 600 district collector offices, much like we were placed in Delhi.

These Zila Swachh Bharat Preraks – personally named by the Prime Minister – were hired, trained and deputed in district and state Mission offices over the course of 2017–18, and did their bit by bringing in the same youthful energy across the system.

Breeding Ground for Innovation

One of the things expected from the youth in the system is innovative and out-of-the-box ideas – new solutions to old problems.

At the state and district level, the ZSBPs brought innovation to the table in an array of work environments. This innovation often took the form of new toilet technologies and innovative solutions to practical challenges faced on the ground. Similarly, at the Ministry, Boss expects us to bring a fresh perspective to every subject under consideration. This has often resulted in brainstorming sessions involving us and other members of the Ministry team that last hours, and which have led to a spark of innovation more often than we can count.

As an example, the idea of recognizing and celebrating the leadership role played by women in the success of SBM was born at one such discussion, and eventually became the Swachh Shakti initiative – an annual event on 8 March, International Women's Day, when the Prime Minister, Chief Ministers and district collectors honour the women champions of the Mission. This has transformed the narrative around women's role as victims of lack of sanitation to a force of positive change in the field.

When Bihar was not matching the pace of progress required for India to become ODF by 2019, the idea for 'triggering Bihar' by infusing swachhagrahis from across the country into the state for a high-intensity behaviour change effort came up in another discussion. This led to the Chalo Champaran initiative, the landmark centenary celebrations of Mahatma Gandhi's Champaran Satyagraha, and gave the state the necessary impetus to reach its goal.

Communicating Effectively for the System

The second big contribution youth in the system have made to the system has been around communicating for the Mission.

At the grassroots, the ZSBPs played an instrumental role in putting together workshops and conferences where district collectors, state mission directors and other grassroots officials were trained on the key priorities of the Mission from time to time. This led to a lot of cross-sharing of best practices and learning from one another amidst states and districts facing similar challenges. Successful districts shared stories of how they got there, and their colleagues gleaned ideas and inspiration from these stories.

At the Ministry, we contributed to several presentations which became a significant tool when it came to communicating the Mission goals, challenges, proposed solutions and the way forward at many critical junctures in SBM's journey. One of us even got an opportunity to join Boss at a Council of Ministers presentation where we presented the roadmap for the Swachhata Hi Seva fortnight for all Union Ministries. The presentation was stark and brutally honest about the gaps in sanitation in various sectors but, more importantly, proposed workable solutions going forward. The highest profile audience in the country listened with rapt attention as Boss made the presentation. At the end, the Prime Minister himself got up and addressed the Council with a powerful message about the imperative to deliver on the outcomes highlighted. He also appreciated the quality of the presentation.

Use of Technology

With youth also comes relatively easier access to and understanding of new technologies, such as the knowledge of social media, apps, online portals and solutions.

When we joined the Mission, its presence on social media was negligible, with a small following on Twitter and Facebook. With support from a development partner, we were able to get a social media agency on board and have been managing its activities on a day-to-day basis since. As a direct result, the followership on social media for SBM-G has grown 100 times in the last three years. The ZSBPs managed the state and district pages which led to a multiplication of communication from the grassroots across the internet.

It wasn't just communicating in cyberspace though. There were also mega events along the way that we supported, which touched several grassroots workers, sarpanchs, swachhagrahis, self-help groups, women champions and cutting-edge functionaries. The ZSBPs, similarly, could be found organizing travel and accommodation for our grassroots champions, as well as compiling feedback from the participants to relay to the highest offices so that we could do better with each event.

Managing Relationships in the System

One of the biggest challenges in a role like this is managing relationships. A youngster from the outside is just that – an *outsider* and admittedly *inexperienced* compared to senior officers – which makes it a precarious position to be in, especially when given direct access to the top office.

The ZSBPs faced several inter-personal challenges in the field. Their very presence in the system was sometimes seen as an incursion by those who felt protective of their turf. There are always elements in any system who benefit from the status quo and see anyone trying to change things as a threat. Navigating local politics was probably the biggest challenge for a ZSBP and it is no coincidence that those who were exceptionally successful in their roles were also exceptionally good at integrating themselves into the system and building friendly relationships with Government colleagues.

At the Ministry, our attitude from Day 1 was to treat everyone at the Ministry with utmost genuine respect for their experience and the accumulated wisdom that comes with it. While the nature of our job sometimes put us in a position of differing with conventional wisdom, it has, thankfully, never led to personal differences. This hasn't been an easy feat to accomplish. We owe much of it to the kindness and forgiveness of our senior colleagues and to Boss's consistent support, but it has also demanded conscious and sustained effort on our side.

This 'relationship management' is something without which the entire concept of infusing youth in the system may have fallen apart. This makes it probably the most important factor for any new initiative trying to replicate this model. The onus for this is on both – the support from the boss (Secretary sir at the Ministry and the Collectors at the district level), as well as the emotional maturity of the youngsters in question.

Joy at Work

Another important role the youth can play is in forging bonds that go beyond the professional by bringing exuberance and joy to the workplace. The long hours we spend at the Ministry are usually double or triple the time we spend at home with our families. Many of the ZSBPs worked almost 24×7. Imagine what a nightmare it would be if we didn't have fun at it!

So we do our bit and we enjoy it. This might mean discussing an interesting book Boss suggests we should read (on our own time – 'Between 3 a.m. and 5 a.m.' as he likes to say!), or weighing out how the World Cup semis may be affected by the outcome of that day's match. Keeping us on course with a bit of encouragement, post some heavy work months, the Boss hosts the team for annual get-togethers at his residence, where the three of us help to organize the games and entertainment as well as the creative mock awards and certificates to give to each member of the MDWS family. While work at the Mission is extremely serious business, these small bouts of fun and games certainly help make the ride more joyful for everyone.

The 'Impossible is Nothing' Gang

Finally, and perhaps most importantly, the biggest contribution the youth can make to a 'Mission (seemingly) Impossible' is their sheer belief that it *is* possible. With great ignorance comes great faith. Unburdened by an in-depth knowledge of failures of the past sanitation missions and programmes in the country, we – as well as the ZSBPs – brought to the table our blind faith in the achievability of the Mission goals and Team Swachh Bharat's capacity to achieve them.

This blind faith that the 'youth in the SBM system' came with was important in the face of the initial scepticism of 2014, both inside and outside the system. To this day, it helps us see the larger positive picture in the face of criticism and nitpicking aimed at the Mission from certain quarters, and forge ahead in our relentless efforts to do better than we did last week, last month, last year. In hindsight, we have learned that Disraeli was on to something – no large-scale change is possible without a bunch of foolhardy people who come together and say, 'Impossible is nothing.'

Swachhata Hi Seva

SANJAY GUPTA

Editor-in-Chief, Dainik Jagran

THE SWACHH BHARAT Mission (SBM) will go down in the annals of Indian history as a movement which not only made a decisive mark on the country's social behaviour, but also demonstrated that if we are determined, the condition and direction of the country can be changed, and that too, quickly.

When SBM was launched, it was seen as a tough challenge, given the vast population of the country and the 'this is just how it is' attitude. As of May 2019, with little less than five years of the programme in play, we can clearly observe an encouraging scenario in the country. Apart from the incredible work done by the administration, the credit goes to the general public and the media which played a critical role in spreading the message of 'swachhata' to the people at large. Those who doubted the success of this mission in 2014 have been forced to reconsider.

The driving force behind the success of this mission is the commitment of the Prime Minister himself. He roused the people by asking fundamental questions about whether it was the job of the cleaning staff alone to keep our country free from filth. Did the 125 crore people of our country have no responsibility towards it. In the recent past, when the Prime Minister washed the feet of five safai karamcharis in Varanasi, it demonstrated his respect for the people engaged in sanitation and the level of his commitment to cleanliness. His very resolute spirit transformed mundane work – from toilet construction to the general cleanliness of public places – into a mass movement. Today, it is clear that cleanliness is becoming a part of everyone's lifestyle. The perception of people towards cleanliness has changed. Throwing garbage recklessly is considered wrong.

Information, Education and Communication (IEC) play a vital role in the success of any programme at the ground level. On 3 October 2014, the day after the launch of SBM, the Prime Minister dedicated his first 'Mann ki Baat' programme to the ideal of 'swachhata'. He underscored the value of the Mission, appealed to the people to join it and presented a blueprint of this resolution.

Since the topic for discussion was of social relevance and contributed to nation-building, all forms of media joined this Mission right from the get go. The duty of the media is to inform, educate and encourage people, and be committed to social responsibilities. On any social topic, newspapers, television channels and other means of communication and contact can create broader awareness, so that the behaviour, thought and attitude of the common diaspora is given a positive direction and social reformation is accelerated. Today, social media has also become a strong means to reach the people, and even the Government is using it.

Social issues have always been an integral part of the editorial policy of *Dainik Jagran*. An educated and healthy society, environmental protection, women's empowerment, water conservation, poverty alleviation, and population management through skill development have been its core issues. The success stories of individuals and organizations associated with these issues encourage large sections of the community to take action for their betterment. The media plays an important role in a democracy by inspiring society to join Government schemes – only then are the best results achieved. No responsible media house can overlook such social interests.

With a spirit of generating discussion on social issues, the media did a great job of fulfilling its duties towards creating large-scale awareness for cleanliness in society, and a consciousness for cleanliness and sanitation even in the far-flung villages of the country. Thousands of people joined hands with Dainik Jagran group as well. The *Dainik Jagran* team had already been engaged in the drive for cleanliness. Be it transferring 35,000 tonnes of garbage from twenty-five cities to disposal sites or the renovation of 4,400 ponds for conservation of precious water, as a guardian of society we have always been conscious of the problems plaguing it. We adopted 1,000 ponds and took charge of enhancing their water storage capacity by de-silting and cleaning them. In different cities of the country, sanitation workers were felicitated personally by prominent personalities. In select cities, school safai karamcharis took the role of guest teachers and taught the students the ways and means to maintain hygiene and cleanliness. Women members of *Dainik Jagran*'s Sangini Club, active in 32 cities, visited their respective domestic helps and made them aware of cleanliness and sanitation.

Dainik Jagran continues to spread word of these drives to its over 7.25 crore readers through news reports. Our family's Trust is also working on sanitation in the rural areas. Today its coverage has reached up to 400 villages.

The sanitation revolution today is proof of how a small action can be transformed into a national mission. While cleanliness may have been discussed in a village, mohalla or at the town level, for the first time, with the Prime Minister placing it at the forefront of the development agenda, it became an issue for the entire country. It was a great achievement that this Mission was controlled directly from the top. The Prime Minister even picked up a broom himself in the Valmiki slum of New Delhi and initiated the Mission in 2014. This act of the Prime Minister might have been considered only symbolic, but the resolve with which he forged the way was amazing.

Every section of the society started joining in. People from the corporate world to Bollywood, Government departments, sports and social organizations, all came forward. It is difficult to recollect if any mission has ever attracted celebrity participation at such a large scale. All over the country cleanliness drives were initiated. The media played a significant role in ensuring that such a large group of people joined this social issue in full force. Today, there is hardly any citizen of the country who is not conscious of sanitation and cleanliness.

Attitude is a great impediment in the creation of a clean society. Today the most important thing is to become a responsible citizen. Why are we not always conscious of cleanliness and sanitation while moving on the road or travelling in buses or trains? The situation is changing now. By making cleanliness a mass movement, the life of 3 lakh children will have been saved on account of deaths avoided due to diarrhoea when SBM declares an Open Defecation Free India.

The fight against filth is long drawn. The tempo of this social movement will have to be maintained in the coming years as well. It is incredible that until a little over four years back while only 39 per cent of rural homes had toilets, today that figure stands at nearly 100 per cent.

Open-defecation-free behaviour will gradually become the norm. We have to remain determined. The people conscious of cleanliness will also have to train the next generation. We will have to continue our efforts to bring cleanliness in the category of social values. For this, social institutions will have to be kept associated at a large scale with the movement, and the media will have to be one of the flag-bearers of swachhata. If this enthusiasm is maintained, if the chain of cleanliness volunteers grows longer and stronger, if our dedication for cleanliness is strengthened further, then no force can prevent India from becoming one of the cleanest nations in the world.

Power of Faith for a Swachh and Swasth Bharat

SADHVI BHAGAWATI SARASWATI

Secretary General, Global Interfaith WASH Alliance

IT IS SAID, 'Faith can move mountains.' With approximately 84 per cent of people in the world and over 90 per cent of the people in India subscribing to faith, it is perhaps the most powerful force we have.

Faith is that which guides and informs our beliefs and therefore our actions. When we united with the Swachh Bharat Mission (SBM), we knew that faith would bring great and lasting change. So it was that the Global Interfaith WASH Alliance (GIWA) took action alongside the Government of India for this crucial cause. Faith has become a robust force in the Swachh Bharat movement.

The Historic Call

In 2014, the Honourable Prime Minister, Shri Narendra Modiji, gave a historic clarion call for a Swachh Bharat. He called upon the people of India to be active co-creators in the condition of their country, to abandon obsolete ideas of cleanliness being someone else's business, and to take up the job of making India swachh, sundar, surakshit and swasth. Shri Modiji put the power back into the hands of the people. With each of us joining hands, hearts, minds and missions, we can make our country clean, healthy and prosperous.

Along with the call for cleanliness, Shri Modiji demonstrated the power of personal action. When he raised not only his voice but also his own hands to sweep the streets it filled the country with ardent enthusiasm: If the Prime Minister can sweep, everyone can sweep! If it's not beneath Modiji, it isn't beneath anyone. This shift from 'anshan' (demonstration) to action was further underscored when the Prime Minister personally helped construct a toilet in Varanasi in 2017.

HH Pujya Swami Chidanand Saraswatiji, the founder of GIWA, has emphasized to the masses, 'When the head of a nation becomes the Pradhan Sevak, serves as a Safai Sevak and has the courage to be a Chowkidar then the entire nation will naturally rise to the call.'

However, in a country of more than 1 billion people, the endeavour to teach, touch and transform the lives of the people of 6,00,000 villages, speaking twenty-two languages and innumerable dialects, was Herculean.

That is where GIWA came in. After decades of unifying and inspiring leaders and communities of all faiths, we realized that faith can also bridge the gap between infrastructure and inner structure, between that which has been provided by the Government and the values and belief systems which determine the people's response. Faith leaders provide us with a moral and social compass, and their words carry unparalleled motivational power.

Uniting the Forces of Faith

The premise upon which GIWA was founded is that our definition of peace must expand. GIWA is committed to a definition of peace that includes refraining from any behaviour that might cause the suffering and/or death of our sisters and brothers of any race or religion. Foremost is the responsibility to protect our nation's – and the world's – rapidly dwindling fresh water resources.

When GIWA first began working with the historic SBM, half of the nation's population was defecating in the open. The myriad reasons spanned from lack of access to lack of capacity to lack of awareness and understanding. Additionally, and quite significantly, hundreds of millions of people simply didn't understand why a toilet was necessary in the first place. When they, their parents and grandparents and everyone they knew defecated outside, why change?

At the time, more children under the age of five were dying in India than anywhere else in the world, mostly due to poor WASH conditions. Nearly 7 per cent of the country's GDP was being lost due to poor WASH, mainly from all the deaths and sick days taken by the millions of men, women and children impacted.

Understanding that it is to faith leaders that people turn for direction, GIWA launched a progressive campaign to motivate, educate and mobilize the masses. In so doing, GIWA brought together leaders of all faiths, political leaders, renowned entertainers, community leaders and many others to motivate the masses to build toilets and embrace their universal use.

Over the next few years, GIWA, in partnership with SBM, UNICEF and others, organized large summits, conferences and motivating panels at huge events in Uttarakhand, Ladakh, Bihar, Assam, Uttar Pradesh, Madhya Pradesh, Maharashtra, and other locations to change the way faith leaders and followers think about sanitation and cleanliness. With slogans like 'Meditation and Sanitation must go together', 'Sanitation IS Meditation', and 'Toilets before Temples', we have been able to align the work of faith with the march towards a Swachh Bharat.

We also created a grand social movement called the 'Swachhta Kranti' (Clean Revolution), which was designed to empower and mobilize the people of India to *be* the change *as an act of faith* ... to commit themselves, tann, mann and dhan, to a swachh, sundar and swasth Bharat.

The inspiration has overflowed into the work of faith leaders across India, as we encouraged them to take up the cause of building toilets and providing clean water and better hygiene. And the inspiration spread to families and communities as they heard the words of their own beloved leaders, which they began to follow like gospel.

Additionally, in order to give people the inspiration, tools and knowledge they need in order to realize their goals, GIWA – along with our many dedicated partners – launched several on-ground initiatives, including World Toilet College, the WaterSchool programme, Women for WASH Initiative, WASH on Wheels travelling roadshows, the Menstrual Hygiene Management Campaign, and much more.

Some of GIWA's recent initiatives are highlighted below:

Major Summits and Mass Events

To realize the goals of SBM, GIWA brought together India's foremost faith leaders for and during mass events. We've inspired millions at all four Kumbha Melas through hundreds of programmes that have seen the participation of revered faith leaders, entertainers and political leaders including the President and Vice President of India. Together, we've led rallying calls for toilets across the nation, in our historic Worship for WASH and Women for WASH Summits, You are the Solution Summits, the Summit of Grace, the Gandhian Resurgence Summit, the Summit of Solutions for the River Ganga, grand kathas, and mass faith events across the nation and around the world. With national, sometimes global, broadcast, our summits and events have impacted the hearts and minds of millions for a clean and healthy India *as a call of faith*.

According to an independent study of GIWA's Swachhta Kranti campaign at the Ujjain Kumbha Mela, for example, an estimated 17.5

lakh people were exposed to and impacted by our messages during just the month-long Mela alone. Millions more were impacted at our recent campaigns at the Prayagraj Kumbha Mela.

ODF Nalanda

In a historic, nearly six-month long campaign, GIWA's team inspired, educated and mobilized the masses in over 300 villages and cities through our unique WASH on Wheels Travelling Theatres. Every day hundreds, sometimes many thousands, were inspired by our puppet shows, audience interactions, screenings of inspirational videos, youth rallies, community leadership meetings and more within their own cities and villages. These grand events were followed by classes held in collaboration with the state government, local authorities and local populations, to directly address the issues that were preventing communities from reaching SBM goals.

During the campaign, it was estimated that over a million people were impacted. In that short span of time, we also educated more than 800 faith leaders, community leaders, teachers, masons and swachhagrahis in classrooms by our instructors. Working with the state of Bihar, we also provided five-day trainings for all of the state's ZSBPs and state SBM Coordinators. We also worked with the state of Bihar and UNICEF to educate scores of jeevika leaders for a ten-day Training by GIWA as Master Instructors for Sanitation Ambassadors.

Shortly after the conclusion of our campaign, Nalanda district was officially declared Open Defecation Free (ODF).

In evaluations hand-completed by over 13,300 respondents

- 97.42 per cent of participants rated the programme as 'Good' to 'Excellent'
- 95.36 per cent of respondents said they were more likely to tell people to always use toilets after participating

- 94.52 per cent of respondents said they were more likely to construct their own toilets after participating.

The World Toilet College

GIWA's World Toilet College was inaugurated in India in 2016, with the mandate of providing the finest of courses, delivered by expert educators. Our aim is to enable community members and professionals to become Change Leaders who can motivate, mobilize and educate people towards successfully and sustainably meeting SBM goals.

In partnership with Reckitt Benckiser's Banega Swachh India and in affiliation with the World Toilet Organization, some 6,500 people have been educated by the World Toilet College, led by GIWA's Secretariat since its inauguration, including Government employees, PHED (Public Health Engineering Department) water engineers, academics, pradhans, swachhagrahis, citizen sanitation ambassadors, masons, environmentalists, jeevika leaders, schoolteachers, faith leaders, and more in workshops and classes designed towards ensuring successful ODF Plus results.

WaterSchool: Educating, Inspiring and Building WASH Facilities

Our WaterSchool programme, in partnership with Swarovski, was launched to educate and inspire the schoolchildren of the Ganga-Himalayas through daily classroom sessions conducted by GIWA educators. In addition, GIWA is actively providing poor and needy schools – particularly government schools – WASH facilities and the repairs they need in order to ensure the health and well-being of all students. These include toilets, handwashing stations, piped water, water-supply cisterns, water-saving gardens, tree planting, emergency infrastructure repairs, and more.

Throughout the year, our WaterSchool programme also organizes special activities that bring schools and communities together for the improvement of their WASH conditions and for the achievement of SBM goals. These include mass clean-ups, tree planting drives, the celebration of special events such as World Water Day, teacher training workshops, participation in mass GIWA summits and more.

- Over 6,000 children have been educated by GIWA's WaterSchool educators since the programme's inception.
- Thousands more have also participated in our mass community participation programmes
- And thousands more have benefitted from GIWA's school-building projects.

Women for WASH

GIWA's Women for WASH programme enables women from villages and slums to become WASH entrepreneurs. Together, they learn to build toilets, handwashing stations and other WASH needs, as well as how to help their neighbours and local schools embrace SBM goals as Sanitation Ambassadors.

Menstrual Hygiene Management Campaign

Proper menstrual hygiene can result in improved health and socio-economic possibilities for millions of women and girls. To enable this, a culture shift is needed, to extinguish harmful stigmas, while enabling the spread of crucial information and the provision of proper facilities.

GIWA, in partnership with Water Supply and Sanitation Collaborative Council, launched a 360 Degree Social Impact Approach geared towards inspiring an end to stigmas while providing crucial instruction for the proper management of menstrual hygiene. This campaign was launched at a massive event in the Prayagraj Kumbha Mela and quickly became widely recognized for the key role it played in inspiring, educating and mobilizing. It will now continue throughout the year in order to inspire tens of thousands more.

The Future Calls

Over the last five years, India has made history. Today, most of the nation can proudly consider itself Open Defecation Free. The statistics of numbers of deaths due to diarrhoea and number of people who defecate in the open are plummeting so quickly that last year's statistics are already outdated. The World Health Organization estimates that over 3,07,000 diarrhoeal deaths in India will have been prevented by 2019 due to the improved sanitation under SBM. For this, our nation should be proud, as should all who made this great and mighty dream an on-ground reality.

However, the war has not been won yet, as our population burgeons and both national and global water resources continue to dwindle. We will all need to stay united to ensure that toilets stay in use, and that further SBM goals, including for solid and liquid waste management, are met.

It is our patriotic duty to continue to strengthen the already great and historic SBM efforts of our honourable Prime Minister, who has already been acclaimed as an Earth Champion, and it's now time for every citizen of India to become an Earth Champion. The power of faith in this mission is tremendous.

The Making of a Great Nation

SADHGURU

Founder, Isha Foundation

HISTORICALLY, WE AS a culture have always invested heavily in both personal and public hygiene. Even today, we stand out as a nation in terms of personal hygiene. Most women will not enter their kitchen without a morning bath. No one enters a temple without a shower. No yogic practice is performed without cleansing the body first.

Taking care of the internal and external cleanliness of the body is a habit that has stayed with us. However, the awareness that we need to keep our public places clean has taken a beating. This has happened because Bharat, under the expert care of colonial guile, decimated itself from being the greatest economy on the planet 25 decades ago. Industries were destroyed. Taxation was back-breaking. This slowly took us to a place where no one had the means, energy or resources to maintain public hygiene.

Unfortunately, even after Independence, governments have not taken enough care to organize cleanliness in the public space. This is not a complaint. Maybe we have had other things to do. Maybe people thought this was not important enough. But today, we know that lack of public hygiene is costing the nation dearly.

Malnourishment and lack of public hygiene generally complement each other. Repeated bouts of bacterial and parasitical infection in the digestive tract take away the ability to absorb nutrients. This is happening to so many children in the country. Considering all this, making India clean is a very important project. I am glad that for the first time, the Prime Minister of the country has taken this up.

When the Prime Minister launched the Swachh Bharat Mission (SBM) on Gandhi Jayanti in 2014, a certain section of society was making comments: 'Why is the Prime Minister talking about pedestrian issues when there are larger issues to be addressed?'

These people do not realize that addressing such pedestrian issues is in our national interest. Without creating a clean nation, developing a nation into a great possibility will be out of question because the infections and other things we carry within us will not allow us to maximize our true potential.

The process of cleaning India is not an overnight job. At the same time, if we can inspire the entire citizenry, it would be quite an easy task. It has to be understood that in this country, nothing changes just by changing policies. It takes an emotional movement, which is what I believe the Prime Minister is trying to do.

Besides the individual's role, today, there are many technologies evolving in the world to transform filth into wealth. There is no such thing as waste in this universe. It is just a question of whether we know how to use something or not. The time has come when we have to learn to transform everything and use it for our well-being. What was earth, we made into filth. We must at least be able to transform it back into earth.

There is substantial knowledge – both traditional and new – on how to do this. We must make the transforming of filth into wealth a part of our national ethos. Every city, municipality and village panchayat must take it up.

For example, a city like Mumbai generates 210 crore litres of sewage per day. Most of it goes to the sea. But if this is treated and used in micro-irrigation, it can water thousands of hectares of agriculture. If you add up sewage from 200 Indian cities and towns, it comes to 3600 crore litres which can micro-irrigate 30 lakh to

90 lakh hectares. Whether it is river pollution, plastic waste or something else, if you show people that what they think is filth can become wealth, you will not find any filth anywhere.

SBM is not just the Prime Minister's movement. It is a crucial step for India to move ahead and truly prosper. Our jawans are standing at our borders, risking their lives every day. Our farmers toil away to feed the nation. Our industrial workers are sweating it out to give us a foothold in the world. One simple way through which we can show our love for our country is by creating a Swachh Bharat.

I'm sure if all of us are determined, we can turn this into a clean nation in twelve months' time. A year is enough to clean up the nation. Let us make this commitment that before Gandhi Jayanti in 2019, we will create a clean India on every level – on the streets, at home, in terms of rooting out corruption, and in our own minds and hearts.

Remember, this is a culture that built consciousness of cleanliness through public drainage systems before any other.

Let us make it happen.

Mission Mode Works

VIJAY KIRAN ANAND

Former Mission Director (SBM-G), Uttar Pradesh

UTTAR PRADESH IS the fourth largest state of India, and the most populous. This means that the state surpasses almost every other state in the country in terms of both scale and complexity of any social challenge. When the Swachh Bharat Mission (SBM) was announced, it was clear that how Uttar Pradesh manages sanitation in its villages and cities would significantly impact our larger national goals. The SBM-Grameen (SBM-G) success story in the state is characterized by strong political will and participation of all stakeholders, right up to the grass-root level.

My experience as SBM Director, Uttar Pradesh, has been enriching, multidimensional and highly satisfying. I got an opportunity to work with a wide range of people, from village champions to experts in the field of sanitation, as well as esteemed seniors who acted as mentors and guided me to implement the mammoth project objectives. It has been a journey of effective leadership of champion district magistrates, chief development officers, district panchayati raj officers and the administrative machinery in general. SBM reflects the power of a community movement, effective project management and efficient monitoring framework at all levels – village, block, district and state. It is a culmination of the efforts of swachhagrahis and volunteers at the village level, talented young professionals at the block level handling behaviour change campaigns, IT-related monitoring/supervision, and district programme managers offering comprehensive ground-level support to the entire administrative machinery all the way till the state Mission level.

How Uttar Pradesh Was Won

Customized training programmes were initiated in each district over and over again with partners and experts in the field such as World Bank, UNICEF, Water Aid and other knowledge partners. Each district had a team of 100 to 300 champions dedicatedly working for the cause.

Compressed Demand

Offering a Government incentive to build a toilet was an important part of the 'triggering' process. However, a sudden surge in toilet demand could overburden the capacity of the administrative system to process incentive payments within a reasonable timeframe, which would have undermined the effort to mobilize communities and trigger toilet demand. The agility shown by the SBM-G team in Uttar Pradesh, and the ownership and involvement of the people led to the concept of 'compressed demand'. This process effectively compresses the demand for incentives by motivating people who are financially capable of building their own toilets to surrender their claim to the Government incentive. This way, the incentive was targeted only towards those who truly needed it.

Compressed demand = (Total Families in GP) - (Families with IHHL + Families financially capable of building their own toilet)

It was a gruelling task, requiring detailed surveys, perseverance and negotiation skills. The initial lists were verified twice: first cross-checked with the national

Ministry's database, then sent back to the communities to ensure that nobody in genuine need had been left out. The final list was formally approved by the village panchayat and subsequently by the District Sanitation Committee, who is responsible for the programme implementation. The end result was a renewed eligibility list, ranging from a compressed demand of 20 per cent in relatively poorer districts to as high as 40 per cent in the relatively prosperous districts.

Community-Led Total Sanitation (CLTS) Played a key role in implementing the Mission effectively by involving and empowering people in the community.

Nigrani Samiti: 30-member teams (10 children, 10 women, 10 men) from each village who were asked to do regular morning and evening follow-ups at places where people usually went to defecate in the open. They were empowered by giving a proper vigilance tool kit that has a whistle, torch, cap and jacket.

Swachhagrahi: The leader of the Nigrani Samiti is trained in CLTS and shoulders the responsibility of making their village ODF. Their progress was reviewed at block and district level through ODF war rooms. They were also awarded monetary incentives when the village is declared ODF and after six months of ODF sustenance.

Building Capacities

The Mission was focussed on bring about behaviour change within the community towards open defecation *prior to* construction of toilets. This required large-scale training and capacity-building initiatives for a host of field functionaries. Examples of these trainings are:

- **CLTS workshops:** Training of ground-level motivators who were then deployed in villages as 'triggering' teams to sensitize the community towards sanitation through interpersonal communication efforts. Incentive structures were created at each level to reward top performers.
- **Training to Safaikarmis, Rozgar Sevaks and Self-Help Groups** on various aspects of SBM to expand the base of the workforce for the mission.
- **Mason trainings:** An estimation of the number of masons required in each village to make it Open Defecation Free (ODF) in stipulated time was carried out. More masons were trained in twin-pit technology by training them on-site. These trained masons were further deployed at each gram panchayat to share their knowledge to other masons and create a large mason force.

Changing Behaviours

Information, Education and Communication (IEC) activities and campaigns like painting, film-making, essay-writing competitions, wall painting on toilets and public infrastructure, LED screen on sanitation van, etc. helped create a lasting impact on the community. These also promoted a sense of competition among villages.

Swachh Kumbh 2019, Prayagraj

In 2018, I handed over the reins to a new Mission Director and took over as Mela Magistrate to prepare for the Kumbh Mela 2019, the largest religious congregation the world has ever seen.

An estimated 24 crore people visited the Mela in the seven weeks from 15 January to 4 March 2019. The Mela provided a unique as well as challenging landscape for demonstrating the national commitment towards sanitation and public health. The theme 'Swachh Kumbh, Surakshit Kumbh' (Clean Kumbh, Secure Kumbh) was perfectly aligned with the vision of the Government of India's Swachh Bharat Mission, focusing upon efficient solid waste management, sanitation and sewage management.

As Mela Magistrate, chalking out the strategy for Swachh Kumbh 2019 was an enormous task for me, which began over a year prior to the mega event. Even the most conservative estimates indicated that a mindboggling amount of waste would have to be handled. Needless to say, sanitation and waste management received top priority in Kumbh 2019. Equipped with support from the state government, the lessons learnt from past Melas and the findings from the pilot interventions tested during Magh Mela 2018, we committed ourselves towards achieving our targets – 'Clean Ganga and Clean Mela', 'Open Defecation Free (ODF) Mela' and odour-free Mela.

For Kumbh 2019, over 1 lakh toilets, with eco-sensitive containment provisions, were strategically located all across the Mela area – covering the akharas, tent city, administrative offices, vending zones, identified open defecation (OD) spots, and heavy footfall–prone locations like bus stands, parking lots and all major approach roads in the city. Adequate number of cesspool vehicles were hired to empty the septic tanks provided with all those toilets which were located within 200 metres from the river bank. Additionally, scientific odour management measures enabled us to achieve clean and odour-free surroundings.

Minimizing litter and garbage on the streets was another major challenge. More than 200 tonnes of trash was generated in the Mela area every day. Over 20,000 trashcans were placed along road sides, ghats, circulating areas, within the camps and all the vending areas. All efforts were made to ensure that no visitor had to walk more than 25 metres to find a disposal bin. Further, 120 tippers (6 in each of the 20 sectors) and 40 compactors were operated 24×7 to collect and transport the waste to the treatment plant. Adoption of modern practices for toilet cleaning and garbage handling ensured zero contact of garbage with human hands.

A Swachhata Sena comprising more than 10,000 sanitation workers and 1,500 village-level sanitation volunteers – swachhagrahis – was deployed to monitor the cleanliness through Information and Communications Technology (ICT)-based hand-held devices. Health, safety and overall well-being of the sanitation workers was paramount for orchestrating the sanitation efforts for Kumbh Mela 2019. Along with the accommodation, anganwadi centres and adequate and nutritious food, gloves, raincoats and masks were provided to each sanitation worker. In addition, all the sanitation workers and volunteers were trained and sensitized through a series of interactive workshops and training programmes.

Along with this, the Mela also provided extraordinary opportunities to build awareness of the role that clean water, sanitation and hygiene play in supporting human health and improving prospects for a better life. This message resonated strongly with the pilgrims, predominantly from rural communities across India. 'Paint My City' campaign and messaging through outdoor media and sanitation mascots were instrumental in conveying the significance of healthy living as well as Ganga conservation to all the visitors.

The Mela's swachhata efforts garnered unprecedented national and international attention on all forms of media, especially social media. The Kumbh Mela of 2019 has shown that no matter how difficult the challenge, the administration's unwavering commitment to swachhata can meet it. Kumbh 2019 was celebrated as the first ever Swachh Kumbh. It set a 'swachh' example for all future Kumbh Melas. I am proud to say that our team converted this challenge into an opportunity to spread the swachhata message far and wide, and ensured convenience to the millions of pilgrims and tourists who attended this largest religious and cultural congregation in the world!

Technology: An Assuming Enabler

NEETA VERMA, DEEPAK CHANDRA MISRA AND SEEMANTINEE SENGUPTA

National Informatics Centre, Government of India

IN LINE WITH the Vedic adage '*Bahujan Hitaay, Bahujan Sukhaay*' ('For the welfare of many, for the joy of many') and inspired by the Father of the Nation, Mahatma Gandhi, the Swachh Bharat Mission Grameen (SBM-G) was launched as a nationwide campaign, with an aim to achieve universal sanitation coverage for India. To help make this goal a reality, Information and Communication Technology (ICT) was used extensively and in an innovative manner, from conception to implementation. Based on the data insights and experiences from previous sanitation programmes, the guidelines for implementation of the programme were framed with adequate flexibility – keeping the geographic specificities in view – and not as a 'one size fits all' approach.

Technology was successfully utilized across the programme, right from the use of a digital solution to monitor the programme's progress, the use of social media, online platforms and collaboration systems to citizen engagement, information dissemination on sanitation best practices, and organization and management of village-level motivator activities.

Digital Platform

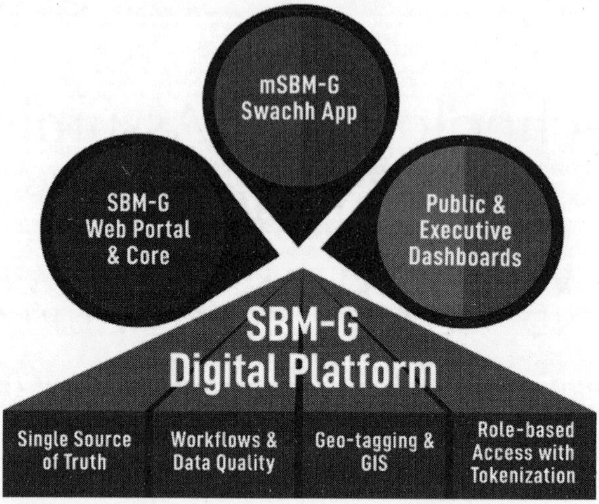

Figure 1: Components of SBM-G Digital Platform

To support the information management needs of SBM-G, a custom web-based platform was conceptualized and made operational by the National Informatics Centre (NIC) – the premier science and technology organization providing informatics services, information and communication technology applications to the Government of India.

The database established by the solution – the Integrated Management Information System (IMIS) – contained up-to-date and real-time information about more than 17 crore households in rural India on various parameters, viz., the status of their household toilet facilities, Open Defecation Free (ODF) status of villages, and the disbursement and consumption of funds, to name a few. This data was regularly updated in a decentralized way by the field functionaries and used to deduce the Key Performance Indicators (KPIs) critical to the success of the programme.

The digital platform acted as a single source of truth whereby all the functionaries of different tiers of the Government – as well as other stakeholders like NGOs, civic bodies, etc. – could monitor the progress of implementation, including financial management and the transfer of funds to beneficiaries. Field-level validations ensured that erroneous data was not entered into the application, and automated approval workflow ensured that data was approved by a competent authority in every district and state.

The solution enabled geo-tagging to monitor the construction of toilets. Mobile apps allowed the capture of geo-tagged images of toilets constructed to verify the progress, location and beneficiary. Over 8 crore (over 87 per cent of all toilets constructed since SBM) of the toilets have been geo-tagged across the country, as of the writing of this piece.

These apps also provided the citizens an interface with Government agencies and allowed sourcing of data directly from the beneficiaries of the programme. This crowd-sourced data enabled Government functionaries to get a glimpse of the ground reality and verify the data fed by the implementing agencies into the SBM-G database. This also facilitated an effective Geographic Information System-enabled dashboard that allowed the SBM-G leadership to monitor the progress vis-à-vis the plan, identify the data sources, analyse the reasons for delays if any, and determine corrective action.

Social Media and the Government's Collaboration Systems

Social media, online platforms and the Government's collaboration systems were also critical enablers in the success of the programme. They were extensively used by the programme managers and grass-roots workers for knowledge sharing and outreach to local communities. Reaching the citizens and getting feedback from the foot soldiers using these technologies had a great impact on policy formulation and programme management.

According to the Global Digital Report 2018, there are 3.196 social media users worldwide, India being among the countries with the largest number of users. For any programme of this scale, the ability to disseminate information and share particular achievements was an important component, which needed a simple, effective strategy. Social networking sites such as Twitter and Facebook served as invaluable tools, communicating information to a wide audience – in the villages as well as cities of India.

SBM-G has its own blog (https://sbmgramin.wordpress.com), Twitter handle (@swachhbharat) with 4,31,600 followers, and a Facebook page (https://www.facebook.com/SBMGramin) with 98,574 followers as on 23 July2019. YouTube and WhatsApp were extensively used for sharing real-life stories and cross fertilization of ideas for successful implementation. Through these, the Ministry of Drinking Water and Sanitation (MDWS) has also been able to publicize its plans, initiatives and programmes across the country, given that almost all states and districts have their own social media sites, and there is large-scale sharing of information.

Social media has helped build the Swachh Bharat brand and increased its visibility by developing relationships and communicating with people involved in sanitation within the country and abroad.

Mass media campaigns – Darwaza Band, Shaucha Singh, mobisodes (mobile episodes) promoting the twin-pit toilet technology – have also been disseminated through social media. Swachh Sangraha is a learning portal where field functionaries and experts share sanitation best practices. These platforms have also enabled sharing of learning, best practices and capacity building.

Instant messaging tools such as WhatsApp and Hike have also provided senior leaders with a direct line of communication with functionaries and volunteers, facilitating faster dissemination of information. WhatsApp groups of officers and field functionaries are generally buzzing through the day with examples of best practices from the ground. Government collaboration systems such as video conferencing and web-casting were also extensively utilized for conducting trainings and capacity-building programmes.

Architectural Resilience

The SBM-G digital platform – a multi-tenant solution – was made operational in early 2014 and has been evolving ever since to meet the changing functional requirements for planning and monitoring. The basic data of toilets is updated by functionaries at the block level (5,921 block users) and other users who update data from districts (697 district users) and the 36 states and Union Territories, using role-based access. Apart from these Government functionaries, the Zila Swachh Bharat Preraks (motivators) at the field level also update the daily status of progress of the scheme and data related to mass campaigns like Swachhata Hi Seva, Chalo Champaran, etc. A total of 2.5 lakh mobile app users access the SBM-G portal on a regular basis. The toilet photographs captured through mobile apps are uploaded on the database along with the geo codes.

In order to get a holistic view of the outcomes, a cross sectoral view of the interventions through various social sector schemes is required. For this, the SBM-G solution inter-operates with other e-Governance solutions – such as Local Government Directory (http://lgdirectory.gov.in) and Mahatma Gandhi National Rural Employment Guarantee Scheme (http://nrega.nic.in) – in addition to some of the state-level systems, which facilitate Direct Benefit Transfer (DBT) for SBM-G beneficiaries.

The solution also interfaces with Swachhata Surveys carried out by third-party agencies, viz., Swachh Survekshan Grameen and National Annual Rural Sanitation Survey (NARSS) applications, as well as the Swachhata Sameeksha application, which facilitates capturing the status of Swachhata Pakhwada plans and activities.

In addition to these, the system inter-operates with the spatial database of administrative boundaries up to the village level. Executive dashboards are available with geographical representation of the data. This level of seamless inter-operability and horizontal linkage with external systems was successfully achieved through use of the data standards.

Way Forward

Technology will remain one of the foremost enablers for SBM-G. The rich data repository created during its implementation will provide a scientific basis for future policy formulation, planning and implementation. As SBM-G evolves, there may be a need to prioritize sustainability of the sanitation value chain, solid and liquid waste management and hygiene practices in subsequent phases. There is a need for increasing emphasis on collection, segregation and safe disposal of solid and liquid waste, and adoption of decentralized technologies like vermi-composting, community biogas plants, low-cost drainage systems based on geographical area, which are socially and technically acceptable and environmentally safe. Value created by the programme in the years to come could be increased significantly through the adoption of advanced technologies such as:

- **Analytics** – A critical component of the programme is to ensure sustainability of usage of toilets by the citizens. Sentiment analysis on the data generated through social media platforms and analytics enabled by big data can be used to derive insights about the enabling factors, leading to sustained use of toilets by the citizens or otherwise and help the state and Central governments make proper interventions, whenever required.
- **Artificial Intelligence** – AI can be used effectively for ascertaining whether data being uploaded on the platform, in the form of images and voice, have conformed to the norms prescribed by the programme managers so that the repository can be effectively leveraged upon to avoid delays in beneficiary payments, service delivery, etc.
- **GIS** – GIS technology can play a very important role in designing the solid and liquid waste management infrastructure of villages. It can help in deciding locations of

drainage systems and biogas plants. GIS can also be utilized to monitor the status of functionality of existing assets created under the programme.

- **Internet of Things (IoT)** – Sensor technology can be used in garbage bins to monitor timely garbage collection and in water pipelines to check water supply status. This technology can be utilized to maintain the assets and will further the sustainability of the programme, as the data collected from the sensors can help in taking right decisions and intervening for proper maintenance of assets as well as service levels.

It is evident that several factors have contributed to the success of SBM-G. Of these, ICT was ingeniously and effectively utilized for creating a mass cleanliness movement. The timely and comprehensive support provided by an agile and resilient technology solution has been one of the critical success factors in facilitating the overall governance process. The policy makers and programme managers have extensively utilized the digital platform for immediate intervention through mid-course corrections in policy and transformation in strategy, by accessing real-time insight into the ground reality.

The use of a common digital platform at the national level, to view and evaluate the implementation progress as well as enable collaboration between different participating stakeholders, was highly effective as it ensured 'anywhere-anytime' availability of authoritative and consistent data. The management of a common platform was not only cost-effective, it also allowed for investment into an architecture that supported high availability of resources and delivered consistently strong performance in a dynamic and unpredictable environment.

Technology was also a critical enabler – as evidenced in the use of social media, online platforms and digital technologies – in engaging citizens; disseminating information of best practices and success stories; and organizing and managing activities of grass-roots functionaries in geographically dispersed locations. All these initiatives resulted in an enhanced level of transparency of processes.

As demonstrated by the experience of SBM-G, each programme poses unique requirements for ICT, and it is incumbent on the technology providers to suggest and support innovative use of technology towards ensuring the programme's success. The success story of this digital platform has inspired many national e-Governance initiatives, and the body of knowledge acquired by NIC can be utilized for many such programmes in times to come.

Toilet – A Love Story

AKSHAY KUMAR

SBM Ambassador

ONE OF THE greatest things about being an actor is getting the opportunity to be involved in causes that can make a difference. Entertaining people might be my passion in life, but making a difference to their lives is where my heart truly lies, and being able to change lives for the better is the most powerful blessing one can ever be given.

I am fortunate to have received so much love and respect for many projects over the years, but none quite as much as for *Toilet – Ek Prem Katha* (*TEPK*)! The makers of the film realized that it takes being a good human to help humanity rather than just preaching without practice, and it took courage to create a film that dealt with what was considered a taboo subject. Many actors had turned down this role, but when the idea was presented to me, I couldn't wait to delve into something so real and so raw. I didn't care who I offended, as long as I could better even one woman's life. All it takes to engineer social change is one brave soul whom others will follow, and that is exactly what happened. Watching the film's protagonists, Keshav and Jaya, build a toilet in their home encouraged countless others to do the same in real life – that was the biggest reward that I could have hoped for from this project.

Since the Prime Minister launched the Swachh Bharat Mission in October 2014, it has done wonders for sanitation across the country. I am so glad that I jumped on board as a brand ambassador and furthered the cause through *TEPK*, rather than admire it from afar. There is no point in just wanting things to improve, you have to *be the change* in order for things to change.

In the movie, Jaya and Keshav, played by Bhumi Pednekar and me, are a feisty couple who fall in love despite many odds and get married. But their happily-ever-after is rudely interrupted when Jaya realizes on the very first morning of their marital life that Keshav's family does not have a toilet at home. And that is where the story of her struggle to reconcile her love for her husband with her need to protect her personal dignity and hygiene begins. Not only does she eventually manage to change Keshav's lackadaisical attitude towards this grave issue, overturn myths, taboos and perceptions around sanitation held by his family and the rest of their village, but she becomes a national icon for women everywhere in India.

Today, reality has imitated reel life, and across the villages of rural India you will find a Jaya who refused to marry into a family that did not have a toilet, or a Jaya who walked out of a marriage to take a stand for her dignity, health and safety. These women have led the Mission from the front lines, and I salute their courage and leadership. We all have a lot to learn from them: they are leading the charge on multiple fronts including the challenge to inequality in the world. Strong women create change, and I could not be more proud to be associated with their story.

While the commercial success of the movie was a great endorsement of my belief in the cause of sanitation, the 'jan andolan' that the Swachh Bharat Mission has led to was also an unwavering signal of what the country wanted and was ready for. To me, it was living proof that the 'swachhata' wave had gripped the nation. The voice of a billion beating hearts was now reverberating across our land.

Strengthened by this realization, I went on to join the Mission as a brand ambassador to promote the twin-pit toilet technology, which I believe is pure economic genius. The twin-pit toilet is completely safe, hygienic and ideally suited to large parts of rural India, and it is recommended by the World Health Organization as well as the Government of India. Research has shown that one of the reasons rural households might hesitate in building and/or using this low-cost technology is the stigma associated with emptying the pit. However, it is scientifically proven that compost made out of the waste collected in a standard twin-pit toilet is not only safe to handle with your bare hands but is a rich fertilizer for use in agriculture. I myself have dug out and emptied toilet pits in many states now, and so I speak to you from personal experience, not a theoretical understanding or script of any nature.

The first pit of a standard twin-pit toilet model fills up in roughly five years for a family of five or six. The waste can then be easily redirected to the second pit, while the contents of the first pit become safe-to-handle compost in six to twelve months, which is rich in NPK (nitrogen, phosphorus and potassium) and ideal for use in agriculture. In many parts of India, this is also known as 'sona khaad' (golden fertilizer) because of its high nutrient content. Bhumi and I did the ad to help spread this important message and I will continue to spread awareness until squatting in private becomes a sustained habit for every household.

Bear in mind that we must all clean our own toilets; this is not the job of the women in our families or something that someone from a particular caste or section of society should have to handle. We all have to rise above these notions. This is the twenty-first century and no one was born to clean after you – so pick up your toilet brush and make your washroom a sanctuary of cleanliness!

It was the strength behind this cause that gave me the confidence to make an even more 'controversial' film later in 2018, called *Pad Man*. This is the true story of a social entrepreneur who produces low-cost sanitary pads to provide rural women access to proper menstrual hygiene, even though it cost him his home and his wife. Even in today's times, the antiquated beliefs associated with menstruation are killing women everywhere. But, like all things that men don't like to talk about, we think that if we pretend it's not happening then it can't really be a problem. Well, it is. And as part of the movement trying to topple the age-old tradition of menstruation denial, I am proud to admit I not only made men talk about it, I made many hold a sanitary pad for the first time in their lives. The best part is not only are men talking about it now, they are helping their daughters and encouraging them to continue education, rather than locking them up at home when they are menstruating and teaching them to be ashamed of having their period.

My message is to all men: Make sure you have a toilet in your home. Ensure that you, your wife, your children, your parents, and everyone else in your home uses it and keeps it clean. No one should have to defecate in the open. Ask your wife about what she goes through during her periods. Ensure that she and every woman in your family uses a safe product during their periods, and not something unhygienic like mud, ash or a dirty cloth. No woman should suffer in silence when we all know that without periods, humankind wouldn't exist. These days, women can choose from a wide range of products, from low-cost sanitary pads to reusable pads and menstrual cups that can be used multiple times, thereby reducing the cost burden on your pocket.

In my conversations with people in the Ministry of Drinking Water and Sanitation, I am often apprised of the many instances in the field where common citizens are championing the cause of ending open defecation, ensuring women's dignity and promoting community health as a personal passion. For example, Katta Padmavathi, a sarpanch from a village in Andhra Pradesh, starts her day at 4.30 a.m. by cleaning her village. Sixty-year-old Maangi Devi, a single parent from Rajasthan, gave precedence to building a toilet for her four daughters over completing her humble semi-constructed home. Tarun Das from Jharkhand built a toilet to protect the health and dignity of his family, even though he had seen open defecation being practised in his village since he was a child. Differently abled Mirda Devi from Udaipur became an example for her entire village when she decided to build her own toilet despite her limited resources.

I recently had a wonderful opportunity to have a one-on-one conversation with the Hon'ble Prime Minister and I asked him about the massive feat achieved by the Swachh Bharat Mission – 9 crore plus toilets constructed, over 5.5 lakh villages becoming open-defecation free in a matter of less than five years! Very rightly, the Prime Minister credited the common man and woman of India for this success. These champions are undoubtedly catalysts of change. They are the pillars on which our nation is developing.

No Longer Accepting the Status Quo

MARK SUZMAN

Chief Financial Officer, Bill & Melinda Gates Foundation

THERE IS A large white board in Secretary Iyer's office. On it, he tracks India's daily progress towards the goal of becoming Open Defecation Free (ODF). Every now and then, whenever a village achieves that status, it goes up on the board. But the number of days left to reach zero keeps going down daily, one by one. It is impossible, then, to attend a meeting at the Ministry of Drinking Water and Sanitation (MDWS) without realizing three things: the Swachh Bharat Mission (SBM) is massively ambitious, it has changed the lives of hundreds of millions of Indians, and the clock is ticking.

The reason leaders like Secretary Iyer and his colleagues at MDWS can hold themselves accountable for results in this way is the remarkable support extended to the programme from the very top to get the job done. The Government has demonstrated through its actions that it is serious about a Clean India.

In the development sector, we talk a lot about the importance of 'political will'. Indeed, it's a requirement for success in every single thing we do. Still, the concept can be elusive. It's hard to define 'political will'. As the saying goes, though, you know it when you see it – and when you see it, it looks a lot like Swachh Bharat.

Partnering with Political Will

Prime Minister Narendra Modi made sanitation the centrepiece of his first Independence Day speech after assuming office in 2014. This was a breakthrough. As he said, 'You must be shocked to hear the Prime Minister speak of the need to build toilets from the ramparts of the Red Fort.'

By linking SBM to Mahatma Gandhi's vision for the nation, that speech made it clear that sanitation was not just a political promise; it was a national duty. The Mission's logo, featuring Gandhi's spectacles, conveys the idea that history is watching – to see Clean India succeed.

Just as important as what India's leaders have said, the Government too has put its money where its mouth is. The $30 billion the Government has invested in SBM has made it possible for the Mission to achieve results where previous, smaller Government-funded sanitation programmes had failed.

But money isn't the only resource the Government has devoted to sanitation. It has also spent significant political capital by working across party lines when necessary to make sure that state and local officials fully support the Mission.

Finally, the Government – notably the Prime Minister himself – has spent an extraordinary amount of time on the issue. He has held at least seven massive public events around the themes of a Swachh Bharat and sanitation, and he receives regular updates about the Mission's progress. For Government leaders to pay this kind of attention to the details of sanitation is simply unheard of.

A Substantive Partnership

Political will isn't the only abstract ingredient in the recipe of successful development. Another theme we can't stress enough is 'partnership'. In this regard, too, SBM has provided an object lesson.

It is very easy to think that you have fulfilled your partnership obligations when you are able to put a few organizations' logos on a website. The Government, however, has taken a much more substantive view of what it means to engage partners.

At the Gates Foundation, we have found the Indian Government to be admirably open to new ideas. SBM's leaders start from the point of view that to accomplish something of this magnitude, they need as much expertise and as much perspective as possible, even if it means sharing some of the credit. They have invited partners from every sector to participate, because they know that each brings particular strengths.

Soon after the Mission was announced, many development partners alerted the Government to the need for attention to faecal sludge management. Just building toilets and persuading people to use them isn't enough. While the preferred toilet technology of the Government for rural areas, the twin-pit toilet, is self-sufficient with regard to treatment of faecal waste, other technologies like septic tanks fill up and, therefore, need concurrent waste management. If that waste isn't collected and treated, the toilets become unusable and pathogens leak back into the environment, undoing all the progress.

As a result of this advocacy, India then became one of the first countries to announce a Faecal Sludge Management National Policy and backed that up with resources to build the treatment infrastructure. In response, many states issued their own policies and set aside state funding as well.

There are many such examples of strong partnerships that made the Mission work. For example, the Government has worked closely with Tata Trusts, which recruited trained experts to work alongside hundreds of district collectors through the Zila Swachh Bharat Prerak programme. SBM has also been on the cutting-edge with the behaviour change messages it uses because it is willing to listen to partners. In the beginning, the programme focused a lot on the fact that open defecation poses a safety threat to women, which is true. However, working together – the Gates Foundation, UNICEF and the Ministry – we learned that these messages subtly discouraged men from listening to them, so the appeal was broadened to include and, indeed, specifically target men for behaviour change around toilet usage. At the same time, the Ministry started highlighting the role of women and children as sanitation champions in communities around India, to make it clear that they have the power to be change agents and leaders in this important national movement.

These strategies are working. Recent national and international surveys have shown that a majority of rural Indians who have access to a toilet use it.

The Urgency of Zero

The all-out assault on open defecation in India reminds me in many ways of the country's success in eradicating polio. Like SBM, the polio campaign's goal was also zero. Not 'less polio', but 'no polio at all'. When you have to get to zero, and when you have to do it in a place as large and complex as India, you have to adopt a systematic stance towards the work – and you have to keep track.

When dealing with polio, India took a clear-eyed view of what an effective campaign would require: vaccinating every single child at least three times, which is challenging when 75,000 children are born every single day. The Government hired 2 million health workers to run the campaign, including some who had to carry coolers with a few vaccines across rivers and over mountains to reach children who'd never encountered the health system before. Celebrities like Amitabh Bachchan participated in public awareness campaigns, and Indians in communities across the country mobilized their friends and neighbours to get their children vaccinated. Eradication was everyone's business. That's why my boss, Bill Gates, said that India's success in wiping out polio was 'the most impressive global health success [he'd] ever seen'.

SBM is similarly impressive. The Government has trained hundreds of thousands of swachhagrahis in rural communities to trigger change and motivate hundreds of millions of Indians towards safe sanitation. It has signed up famous actors and cricketers to raise people's awareness. It even put the Mission on Indian currency (refer to the Swachh Bharat logo on all currency notes). All this is necessary, because the same child who received a polio vaccine for the first time also needs to be reached by SBM. And the meaning of the word 'reached' is broader when it comes to sanitation. The polio vaccine is a single drop and you're done, whereas SBM requires behaviour change coupled with a huge infrastructure build, which is harder and takes more time. And yet, after little over four years, India is on the threshold of achieving its goal.

Finishing the Job in India and Around the World

As Gandhi's 150th birth anniversary and the deadline for India to become Open Defecation Free approaches, it is important to celebrate what SBM has accomplished. But, in keeping with the result-oriented culture of the Mission, I also want to conclude with some thoughts on what must come next in India's sanitation revolution.

The immediate priority is not just to finish the job but to make sure it stays finished. Open defecation has been customary since the beginning of time. Meanwhile, for the 600 million Indians reached by SBM, the idea of using a toilet is less than five years old. The Government will need to continue spreading the message of why sanitation is so important – and it will have to continue to be creative and flexible about which messages are most effective – to ensure that India remains Open Defecation Free.

In addition, the Government and its partners, including our Foundation, must focus on innovations in faecal sludge management. A number of related technologies are being tested to serve the specific needs of remote villages, as well as thousands of large dense villages and urban cities and towns. India needs to get these technologies to all the people who are using toilets for the first time.

The second priority is gathering the lessons learned from SBM and sharing them so that other countries can replicate India's success. Over a billion people around the world still don't have access to basic sanitation facilities. As the largest sanitation programme in the world, SBM can serve as a laboratory of effective solutions.

India took an important step in this direction by hosting the Mahatma Gandhi International Sanitation Convention in 2018. Organized by the Government, the convention brought together representatives from 70 countries, including 55 Ministers of sanitation, to discuss the key issues facing the sector.

Perhaps the most important lesson they learned, however, was when the four-day event was opened by India's President and closed by its Prime Minister. Sanitation programmes can work. SBM proves it. But they'll never get off the ground until leaders make it plain that their country can no longer accept the status quo.

Swachh Bharat and the Ripple Effect

HENRIETTA H. FORE

Executive Director, UNICEF

THE MOST ENDURING development victories are not those that are imposed, but those that are embraced by communities, carried forward and made an intrinsic part of people's daily lives. When people decide to change their behaviours, they set in motion a ripple of progress that spreads from child to parent, household to household, neighbourhood to neighbourhood, community to community. India's Swachh Bharat Mission (SBM) to end open defecation practices is a remarkable illustration of this phenomenon. By all accounts, this represents an unprecedented behaviour-change programme in development history, reporting over 500 million people now living in Open Defecation Free villages in 42 months.

Prior to SBM, 12 per cent of the world's population practised open defecation. They often had no choice: their communities lacked even the most basic toilet services. In fact, one in three people – 2.3 billion in all – lacked even a basic toilet or sanitation service. Thanks to the leadership of Prime Minister Narendra Modi, who launched SBM in 2014, India now stands as an inspiring example to other countries travelling the same path to end open defecation – still one of the world's great development challenges.

The lack of toilets and other sanitation services is just one part of the problem. In many communities, open defecation is seen as an acceptable practice – a cultural norm that has endured over generations, despite the enormous risks to people's health and lives.

Indeed, open defecation and poor sanitation extract a significant human cost. For children it can mean illness and death from disease. They are also at risk of stunted growth because of faecal contamination in drinking water, leading to diarrhoea, worm infection and other diseases, damaging their guts and leading to malnutrition in their earliest years. Girls are often kept home and not allowed an education because schools lack separate toilets or proper sanitation. As always, the poorest and most disadvantaged children and families are affected most. This locks them into an intergenerational cycle of risk to their health and their futures.

The tragic human cost is matched by the steep economic cost to societies. According to the World Health Organization, poor sanitation results in an estimated global GDP loss of $260 billion annually, because of related health costs and productivity losses.

At the same time, the benefits of improved sanitation are significant. A 2017 study by UNICEF found that within open-defecation free environments, Indian households can save up to Rs 50,000 per year thanks to medical costs averted and time saved.

Countries simply cannot afford to miss out on this important development opportunity.

Guided by these clear health and economic benefits, India launched the Swachh Bharat Mission in 2014. Its goal was to finally make this accepted practice of open defecation unacceptable. The Mission's success has been undeniable. Since its launch in 2014, the Government of India reports that over 500 million people in rural and urban areas have gained access to toilets. In rural areas, coverage has more than doubled from 39 per cent in 2014 to 99 per cent at the beginning of 2019.

To put this in perspective: sanitation coverage has increased more in the last four and a half years than it did in the preceding 67 years since India's independence in 1947.

This achievement is even more impressive when we consider the longstanding, interlocking barriers that stood in the way for generations of Indian communities. Open defecation has long been an accepted behavioural practice in communities across the country. Cultural taboos prevented the building of toilets near homes. And enduring poverty kept hundreds of millions of people from accessing the facilities they need and deserve.

In an amazingly short timeframe, SBM successfully broke down these barriers by mobilizing every part of Indian society behind it, including communities, families, all sectors of Government, religious leaders, entertainment and sports stars, and businesses. In keeping with the vision of making sanitation 'everyone's business', SBM brought together various development sectors, in order to support better progress in not only sanitation, but education and health as well. Schools need handwashing facilities and separate toilets so girls can manage their menstrual cycles and still attend classes. Clinics and hospitals require clean, sterile environments to prevent infection and disease. Households and communities need toilets to prevent contamination and the spread of illness.

Global development partners also gathered around this important effort, lending their experience, reach and advice as India embarked on this Mission. Together, we are working closely with Ministries to help them integrate hygiene and sanitation across local systems for nutrition, health and education, to reach every community and every family.

Supported by UNICEF, the Word Bank, WaterAid and other agencies and NGOs, the Government focused its investments in areas of greatest need, including high-burden states like Uttar Pradesh and Bihar.

On the corporate front, companies like LIXIL, Unilever, Johnson & Johnson, and corporate philanthropies like Tata Trusts have lent their expertise and investment to this effort, supporting community and school-based sanitation programmes and menstrual hygiene management programmes across India.

SBM also opened the door to innovations, including new toilet designs in disaster- and flood-prone states like Assam and Gujarat. A series of simple design changes keeps these toilets functional even during emergencies, minimizing the risk of disease transmission.

Innovative financing, in this respect, played an important role, by developing alternative credit models to provide affordable loans for households to build toilets. Initially launched in Maharashtra in partnership with Water.org and public and private financial institutions, these loans are now being expanded to Madhya Pradesh and Odisha.

To attract greater investment in this cause, the Swachh Bharat Kosh fund was established in 2014, raising more than Rs 8.7 billion in just four years, thanks to the generosity of companies and philanthropists all dedicated to ending open defecation.

The real secret to SBM's success is more than just 'building more toilets', or policy reform or funding and investment. It is ensuring that people in communities are using these toilets, changing their behaviours, and convincing their neighbours, friends and family to do the same.

From the start, SBM was designed and rolled out as a *jan andolan* – a people's movement. While the Government's commitment and various funding sources are essential, the true heart of the initiative is an army of volunteers, including women, youth, and frontline workers. From densely populated urban slums to tiny, remote villages, these dedicated agents of change went into communities to work directly with families and leaders to convince them of the need to end open defecation.

Especially inspiring were the children and young people who adopted this cause as their own. Some 20 million wrote letters to the Prime Minister informing him of the action they had taken in their communities. In India's Kabirdham district, 1,38,000 students from over 1,700 schools wrote letters to their parents to request that toilets be built in their homes, and the district declared itself ODF soon after. Just last year, over 4,00,000 students registered for the Swachh Bharat Summer Internship, through which they contributed to setting up sanitation infrastructure and worked directly in communities to change behaviours and attitudes. As SBM proves, children and young people are ready, willing and able to be change makers – and change *leaders* – in their communities.

This is where SBM's 'ripple effect' comes in. As more people of all ages become involved, community demand grows. Local governments and decision makers discover a powerful and popular political incentive to continue investing in the issue and ensure that every community – from rural villages to crowded urban areas – has effective sanitation systems, along with safe water supplies.

Leaders have realized that training and employing local, community-based workers to install and maintain water and sanitation infrastructures can have a positive economic impact in impoverished areas. This sets in motion a cycle of progress and opportunity in the communities that need it the most. For example, UNICEF and the Tata Institute of Social Sciences joined forces to train cohorts of skilled sanitation specialists every year, the majority of which are women. They're learning how to manage water, sanitation and behaviour-change programmes in communities. In fact, water and sanitation is an opportunity to help more young people, in more communities, gain vital skills and knowledge that they can carry with them in the years to come.

As sanitation increasingly becomes a social norm in every city, village and rural community, the demand for quality, well-managed systems will grow. According to the Toilet Board Coalition, the market for toilet-related products and services in India is predicted to double to $62 billion by 2021. In other words, this sector represents a significant opportunity as young people consider their future job prospects, especially in poor and disadvantaged areas.

This ripple of progress that has affected communities across India can also extend far beyond its borders, inspiring other countries to follow India's example.

SBM's many achievements were showcased when India hosted the Mahatma Gandhi International Sanitation Convention in 2018. This four-day event brought together delegates from over 70 countries. It was deeply inspiring to see countries gathering to share experiences and best practices in their journeys to ending open defecation.

The conference reminded us that we, as a global community, have much to celebrate – but more importantly, much to do. The last mile of any journey is the most difficult. Without urgent acceleration of our efforts around the world, many countries will not reach the 2030 goal of sanitation for all.

But the conference also reminded us that, embedded in the progress that nations like India have made, we can find the seeds of how to achieve true, lasting *global* progress. As countries live up to their commitments and targets under Sustainable Development Goal 6, the world can learn from India's approach and find similar ways to put community empowerment and ownership at the heart of national plans to end open defecation.

Changing behaviours, constantly improving products, operation and maintenance, and drawing more partners, ideas, support and dedicated national resources to our important cause by building movements that can ripple across communities, countries and entire regions will be the path to success. SBM, in its grassroots-focused approach, is very much a model of sustainable development in action – taking action together now, for the future.

In the words of Mahatma Gandhi, the inspiration for this movement: 'The future depends on what we do in the present.'

The country he loved so well has taken Gandhi's words to heart. The time has come now for other countries to follow India's inspiring example to end open defecation, and finish the last mile of their own journeys towards health, progress and prosperity for all people – including our future generations.

PEOPLE'S PARTICIPATION

Inspired by the Prime Minister's vision of participative development, the Swachh Bharat Mission went from being a Government programme to a national movement of the people, by the people and for the people. Millions of Indians from diverse socio-cultural and economic backgrounds came together for a common cause, making sanitation everyone's business.

Everybody's Business

P.K. SINHA

Cabinet Secretary, Government of India

THE DREAM OF a Swachh Bharat was articulated by the Prime Minister, but for it to become reality, it had to be shared by everyone in the country. For swachhata to replace the lack of sanitation and modify habits ingrained for centuries, a new norm would have to be established. All 130 crore people across 6 lakh villages, 700 districts, 35 states and Union Territories, speaking 22 official languages and 720 dialects from an array of diverse cultures, would have to become stakeholders, and make a change towards swachhata in their own lives.

But a transformation on such a massive scale could not have been the responsibility of one or two Government departments alone. Getting every citizen involved in the Mission would require concerted efforts from all quarters. The ordinary citizen would have to see that swachhata was being prioritized in all spheres, from schools to hospitals to markets to highways and everything in between. Prominent citizens would have to turn influencers and be the torchbearers of the swachhata message. Businesses would have to bring in their creativity and management acumen to propel the Mission forward. Faith leaders would have to preach about swachhata. National and international developmental organizations would have to prioritize swachhata as the cornerstone of holistic development. To put it simply, for swachhata to become a revolution, it would have to become *everyone's business*.

The journey of swachhata as we know it has been a phenomenal and collaborative effort. With the Prime Minister setting the goal of a Swachh Bharat on the not-so-distant horizon, creating ownership of the Mission through a collaborative approach became among the most important tasks on the agenda for the Government of India. While the Ministry of Drinking Water and Sanitation (MDWS) was the nodal Ministry of the programme, every other Ministry had to ensure that swachhata became an integral part of its ethos and manifested itself on the ground in the sectors they governed.

The Government of India ensured that different Ministries and Departments worked together with unified initiatives to instil swachhata across sectors and areas of implementation. As of June 2019, a number of initiatives have been floated and implemented at the Centre under the vision of 'Everyone's Business'. Initiatives like Swachhata Pakhwada, Swachhata Action Plan (SAP) and the Inter-Ministerial Committee were launched with instructions and directions from the Prime Minister himself. These programmes received massive support and response from all Union Ministries and Departments of the Government.

Swachhata Pakhwada

> 'As the Swachh Bharat Mission commenced its journey, it was felt that action should not remain confined to the Sanitation Ministries and Departments. All parts of the Government have to proactively contribute to realize this aspiration along with the public at large.'
>
> – Narendra Modi, Swachhata Pakhwada Yearbook 2016

Swachhata Pakhwada, yet another brainchild of the Prime Minister, is an eminent example of collective action in the

Government. It commenced in April 2016 with the objective of mainstreaming swachhata within the non-sanitation Ministries and Departments, with each of them dedicating a fortnight, once a year, towards innovative, substantial and sustainable swachhata initiatives in their respective sectors. Over the years, the initiative has grown from strength to strength under the leadership and guidance of senior ministers and officials.

A Swachhata Pakhwada calendar is prepared and circulated among all Union Ministries and Departments at the beginning of each year. At any point in time, a couple of Departments celebrate their Pakhwadas where they take up countrywide initiatives to enhance swachhata through their field offices, autonomous bodies, CSR/PSU partners, organizations and most importantly in the sectors under their jurisdiction. To incentivize good performance, many Ministries and Departments give out Swachhata Pakhwada Awards for the best offices, organizations and sections within their jurisdiction. Additionally, the best performing Ministries and Departments are awarded by MDWS.

The Pakhwada activities, rather than being confined to office premises, have reached all the corners of the country, and not just by the efforts of the Departments directly involved with the sector. In September 2017, under the Department of School Education and Literacy Pakhwada, 3 crore schoolchildren wrote letters to their parents demanding to have a toilet at home.

Swachhata Action Plan (SAP)

The Government of India and the state governments together have made direct investments of over Rs 1 lakh crore in the sanitation sector these last five years. Additionally, each Ministry has pledged specific resources towards their Swachhata Action Plan (SAP) – an effort to mainstream sanitation and swachhata in all sectors on a continuous basis.

'It is indeed great to know that 76 Ministries and Departments have come forward to take up swachhata effort under the new initiative, Swachhata Action Plan (SAP).'

– Narendra Modi, SAP Book 2017–18

The SAP was formally launched on 1 April 2017 with the active participation of 72 Union Ministries and Departments of Government of India, who have cumulatively pledged over Rs 35,000 crore towards their respective swachhata plans during 2017-19 to make swachhata an integral element in their existing and new schemes and programmes. The SAP has seen a multi-dimensional range of activities including the adoption of villages, support for sanitation infrastructure, solid and liquid waste management (SLWM), cleaner monuments, school sanitation, better sanitation in hospitals, highways, railways, markets and iconic places, among others. The Ministries have exceeded themselves and implemented innovative and outcome-based swachhata activities.

Some of the broad range of activities conducted under the SAP are as follows:

- River rejuvenation projects and mini watersheds by the Department of Defence Production
- Community and household sanitation infrastructure, SLWM and water restoration in villages by the Ministry of Rural Development
- Biogas plant or power plants by the Department of Animal Husbandry, Dairying and Fisheries
- National biogas and organic manure programme by the Ministry of New and Renewable Energy
- Solid waste management and waste-to-energy initiatives by the Department of Space

- Installation of bio-toilets in trains by the Defence Research and Development Organization and the Ministry of Railways
- Clean plants and clean factories by the Ministry of Steel
- Restoration of water bodies by the Ministries of Petroleum and Natural Gas, and Coal
- Rain harvesting system by the Ministry of Electronics and Information Technology.

Inter-Ministerial Committee (IMC)

To further reinforce the mainstreaming of Swachh Bharat Mission (SBM) across all Ministries and Departments, and create a strong monitoring mechanism, an Inter-Ministerial Committee was formed in 2016. The role of the Committee is to assess and guide the Swachh Bharat initiatives undertaken by the Union Ministries and Departments apart from Swachhata Pakhwada and the Swachhata Action Plan. The members of the Committee represent the key Ministries of Drinking Water and Sanitation, Housing and Urban Affairs, Information and Broadcasting, School Education & Literacy, and Women & Child Development. The members meet every month and present their initiatives and collaborative efforts towards Swachh Bharat, resulting in innovative initiatives like the Swachh Petrol Pump App, Swachhata National Parks, Swachh Swasth Sarvatra [an inter-Union Ministerial joint initiative between MDWS and the Ministry of Health and Family Welfare that provides Water Sanitation and Hygiene (WASH) training to the health workers of Public Health Centres (PHCs)/Community Health Centres (CHCs)] and the Kayakalp programme (wherein the Ministry of Health and Family Welfare is providing monetary support for WASH and hospital infrastructure at the PHC/CHC level).

Today, almost all petrol pumps and toll plazas on national highways have been fitted with gender segregated toilets with regular maintenance and review systems. Across the country, government school toilets are being maintained with a designated and proper maintenance fund. All major ports, agricultural mandis, and tourist and cultural heritage centres have become swachh and green.

Such initiatives are well accepted and have become regular features for the Government. These efforts have allowed Ministries and Departments to discharge their regular functions better, and have had a significant positive spin on their regular programmes. Almost all major flagship programmes of the Government of India have benefited from the improvements in swachhata. Schooling and health outcomes have improved; measures for women's safety have been enhanced; our villages, towns, streets, markets, schools, hospitals, public places are cleaner, and India's image on the global stage has become significantly better. Swachhata has become the embodiment of collective action for development. It is a movement of all, by all and for all – truly, everyone's business.

The Glass Full

BIBEK DEBROY

Chairman, Economic Advisory Council to the Prime Minister

A HALF-EMPTY GLASS versus a glass half-full – it's a cliché. Typically, where is the glass located when you glance at it? More often than not, it is on a table of some sort, below your line of vision. Therefore, your eye focuses on the empty bit. I wonder how we would react if the glass were placed above our line of vision, so that we looked, at it from the bottom, rather than the top. This strikes me as an apt analogy because of a recent incident.

An acquaintance had dropped in, to complain and lament about cabbages and kings. This was the time of the year when assorted diaries find their way on to my desk. Increasingly, people don't use such diaries, but old habits die hard. A beautiful diary (and an accompanying calendar) brought out by the Ministry of Drinking Water and Sanitation, with a focus on the Swachh Bharat Mission (SBM), especially its Grameen (rural) part, lay on my table. SBM was started on 2 October 2014. A little bit about SBM's dashboard first. Since October 2014, 92.5 million toilets have been constructed and 157.3 million rural households have toilets as of June 2019, that is 99.08 per cent of rural households. Just so one has a sense of what this entails, when SBM started, the coverage was 38.70 per cent. Goa and Odisha are the only two states that lag by a bit as I write this;

for Odisha, as is only to be expected, there are disparities between districts. Some districts like Kalahandi, Mayurbhanj, Kendrapara, Malkangiri and Nayagarh pull the state down. Barring these two states, IHHL (individual household latrine application) coverage in all states is in excess of 95 per cent. By October 2019, coverage should be universal. Whichever way you look at it, this is nothing short of a revolution.

All this has a bearing on Sustainable Development Goal 6.2: 'By 2030, achieve access to adequate and equitable sanitation and hygiene for all, and end open defecation, paying special attention to the needs of women and girls and those in vulnerable situations.' Often, in scenarios where open defecation figures prominently and many households are mentioned as not having access to toilets, one finds references to India. For instance, World Bank reports for 2015 note that 40 per cent of the Indian population resorts to open defecation. This is an official World Bank figure.

A December 2018 paper, co-authored by World Bank researchers, states, 'A staggering 48 per cent of Indians continue to defecate in the open despite large-scale efforts from the government to raise awareness about the harmful aspects of open defecation and subsidize latrine construction, and growing latrine ownership. This is a formidable challenge since almost 70 per cent of rural Indian households currently do not have access to improved sanitation facilities.'

Whom do we believe? Numbers like those from the World Bank or the SBM dashboard? Both propositions are true. The reason for apparently contradictory numbers is obvious – cross-country data quoted is often for 2015. And since 2 October 2014, a silent revolution has changed this aspect of rural India. A pity it is silent, a pity it is not recognized much more, a pity cross-country numbers aren't updated sufficiently quickly.

As of June 2019, 618 districts, 6,029 blocks, 2,47,640 gram panchayats and 5,62,000 villages have been declared Open Defecation Free (ODF). A declaration means nothing. Shouldn't there be some verification? Precisely. Out of the 5,62,000 villages declared ODF, 4,94,625 have been verified to be ODF. So what? Toilets have been built. However, households don't use them. Perhaps the toilets don't have water. Perhaps a village is declared ODF, but slips back. These are legitimate questions to ask. And the only way to answer these questions is through a survey. The second National Annual Rural Sanitation Survey (NARSS 2018–19) was conducted by an independent verification agency between November 2018 and February 2019 as part of the World Bank support project to SBM-G. (There was an earlier survey in 2017–18.) NARSS 2018–19 results are still provisional, they have to be finalized. Nevertheless, the provisional results are quite a revelation and need much greater dissemination. As per the survey findings, 93.1 per cent of rural households have access to toilets; 96.5 per cent of people who had access to toilets used them; 90.7 per cent of verified ODF villages were confirmed as ODF. In passing, 95.4 per cent of villages had minimal litter and stagnant water. For the record, these numbers are better than those in NARSS 2017–18. I must confess, they are far better than what I would have expected a priori. Using the glass image, there is some emptiness, but it is a sliver. There is some slippage, but not as much as one might have thought. I am inclined to think the glass is much more than half-full. It is pretty close to being full-full.

So that one is methodologically clear about what this survey entails, 'An ODF-verified village is confirmed to be ODF if, during the survey, it is found that: All households and all public institutions surveyed are found to be using safe technology for disposal of feces and no visible feces found in the village surroundings.' A village may not be confirmed as ODF because of any of the following reasons. '1. Lower than 100 per cent access to toilets in the village; 2. Presence of unhygienic/dysfunctional/unsafe toilet in any household in the village; 3. Non-usage of a toilet by the household members; 4. Non-access of a toilet in schools or anganwadis; 5. Presence of visible fecal matter in the village.' Sure, this is a survey and not a census. Even in an ODF confirmed village, a media report may appear about some household resorting to open defecation, or not using a toilet. That's neither here nor there. Within the parameters of a survey, such improvements boggle the mind.

Such revolutionary changes don't occur merely because the Union or state governments decide to take some action. At best, governments can only be a trigger, a catalyst. Behavioural change confronts the bane of inertia, reminding us of Newton's Second Law of Motion. We do need an external stimulus to change the state. That might be through films like *Toilet: Ek Prem Katha*, *Halkaa* or *Gutrun Gutargun*. Or that change might come from swachhagrahis.

The diary I mentioned has twelve lovely cartoons. One of these is on swachhagrahis. The diary tells us 'Swachhagrahis are the foot soldiers of the Swachh Bharat Mission. Over the last four years, a cadre of over 5,00,000 swachhagrahis has been created who have triggered lakhs of villages to become ODF.' My acquaintance hadn't heard of swachhagrahis until he flipped through the diary on my table. He was so engrossed in lamenting about interest/exchange rates, ships and sealing wax that he, like many citizens of urban India, had failed to notice a silent revolution sweeping through rural India. Let me quote from the August 2018 circular on revised guidelines for swachhagrahis. 'As you are aware, Swachh Bharat Mission (Grameen) [SBM-G] emphasises on intense behaviour change campaigns including inter-personal communication for achieving sustainable sanitation outcomes. Swachhagrahis are the foot soldiers of SBM-G and the motivators for bringing about behaviour change with respect to key sanitation practices in rural areas. Role of swachhagrahis is one of the key factors in achieving the ODF status and sustaining it through post ODF activities. A swachhagrahi is a volunteer who can come from any background, including a local ASHA worker, ANM, anganwadi worker, and staff, water line man, pump operator, member of NCO/CSOs, youth organisations or from the general public living in villages.' Beyond the obvious, there are several things swachhagrahis do – geo-tagging toilets, verifying household behaviour, converting old toilets and retro-fitting them, and engaging in other forms of cleanliness.

In April 2018, the Prime Minister addressed a national convention of swachhagrahis – as part of the Satyagraha Se Swachhagraha programme – and gave awards to ten outstanding performers. Indeed, they are the ones who provide the drive to SBM. They are the ones who have raised the level of the table. We can look at the glass from below and not from the top and say, 'The glass is full.'

My Village, My Pride

RADHIKA SUNDARAMOORTY

Swachhagrahi

'THE PESSIMIST SEES difficulty in every opportunity, but the optimist sees opportunity in every difficulty' is the quote that drives me always. Born and brought up in an economically weak family in Tiruvannamalai district in Tamil Nadu, I have faced several hurdles in my life. After passing the eighth standard, I could not continue my studies due to my family's financial situation. To share the burden of my family, I began working for daily wages, utilizing any opportunity that came my way. However, I was always waiting for a chance to make a significant difference for my family and community.

The year 2004, when I began actively engaging in self-help group activities, was a turning point for me. These groups held various positions in the panchayat-level federation (PLF). Having lost my siblings at a very young age to malnourishment and poor immunization, I started helping pregnant women in the villages so they would receive routine immunization, undergo regular check-ups and take the right medication during pregnancy.

Every person gets a chance to win in his or her life and I was not left behind. In 2012, I got an opportunity to become a Community Resource Person (CRP) through the PLF, where I was given the responsibility to disseminate information on rural livelihood activities, including sanitation to the people in my village. Little did

I know this was only the first step. A revolution was stirring in rural India and, in 2015, I became a part of its supporting base – I was selected to be a swachhagrahi for my village panchayat, Irumbedu panchayat of Arani block in Tiruvannamalai.

I attended trainings on the Community Approach to Sanitation (CAS) at the State Institute of Rural Development (SIRD), which transformed my life. This basic training created a great impact on my approach to rural livelihood activities, and made me realize that access to safe sanitation facilities must be the foremost priority for every individual.

The CAS training taught me about the importance of bringing about effective behavioural change in people to keep them from defecating in the open. I soon realized that a change in behaviour begins with a change in heart. I decided to gather a group of women and children and narrated to them the ill-effects of open defecation, and persuaded them to construct a toilet at home.

In the beginning, progress was slow and I was not happy with it. Around the same time, I found that many women in my village around the age of forty were suffering from urinary tract infections and various uterine problems, and were compelled to remove their uterus through surgery. This took a toll on them, both physically and mentally. I took this as a major point of discussion in gram sabha meetings and made the villagers realize that the underlying cause was simple – the necessity of refraining from relieving themselves until sunset. I also educated them about how the worms in faecal matter, when not disposed safely, could damage the development of the uterus in adolescent girls, affecting their fertility. I then went on to inform them how the diseases contracted because of open defecation could seriously impact the growth and development of a foetus in the mother's womb, even resulting in miscarriage at times. And finally, I made them aware of how malnutrition stemming from repeated bouts of diarrhoea caused by open defecation affects the physical and mental growth of children. These worked as powerful triggers and motivated the villagers to construct toilets at their homes and safeguard their health.

In 2017, the Ministry of Drinking Water and Sanitation organized Swachh Shakti in Gandhinagar to celebrate International Women's Day on 8 March. They invited women sarpanchs and swachhagrahis from across the country. I was one among the participants who went on an exposure visit to Gujarat. This visit was really an eye-opener and educated me on various aspects of how a village may achieve and sustain Open Defecation Free (ODF) status. Thinking of grooming me as an active participant to bring about a change in the society, the then Zila Swachh Bharat Prerak of Tiruvannamalai fuelled me with innovative thoughts and encouraged me to put my creative ideas to action.

With my experiences in the field, I understood that thus far people had not been taught to practise safe sanitation at a young age. With this in mind, I began visiting anganwadi centres and schools, where I taught young children the 'Ten Commandments for healthy living', placing special emphasis on personal hygiene and safe sanitation. I did this so that these messages would make an impression on them at an early age and stay with them as they grew older. These children would then go home and persuade their parents to construct and use toilets, and ensure that overall hygiene and health standards in the household were maintained.

There was also this one instance when, after a long gap, I visited Thellar Government High School for a follow-up session. I was told by a student who was studying in class ten that she had convinced her parents to construct and use a toilet regularly. These words from a young energetic girl gave me true joy and happiness, and galvanized me to work even harder to achieve the goal of a Swachh Bharat.

Some people would tell me that it was expensive to construct a toilet. I wanted to make them realize that their investment in a toilet would fetch handsome returns in the form of savings. After all, good health is too valuable a commodity to compromise on, and I needed to communicate this effectively to my community. I continued to search for innovative ways to communicate to the people how they could construct their toilet in an efficient and cost-effective manner.

An idea eventually came to me when I was invited for an awareness session on sanitation, organized for the students of Government Engineering College, Thatchur. Halfway through the session, propelled by the interest of the students, I drew a model of a twin-pit pour flush toilet with a junction chamber on the ground, differentiating the pit in use with yellow flowers and the other pit with waste tea and coffee packs available at that time. This made a visible impact among students on how the twin-pit toilet works. The students started spreading the message to their parents and neighbours, and promoted toilet usage in their respective villages.

After a lot of effort, a majority of households in my village had constructed toilets and were using them regularly. However, there were still a few households which continued to function without a toilet. I showed the community how the benefits of safe sanitation would accrue only if it was universal. If even one household defecated in the open, it would impact everyone's health. I gathered the community members and went on a door-to-door awareness expedition, ensuring that every household had at the very least started the construction of Individual Household Latrines (IHHLs). It makes me very proud to share that with constant, dedicated effort, in February 2018, my village was declared Open Defecation Free.

Appreciating my efforts, the then project director and the present project director of District Rural Development Agencies encouraged me to share the message with nearby villages, help them achieve ODF status and ensure that all the toilets were used regularly. I started camping in a village for three days where I did the morning and evening follow-ups, triggered the community and monitored toilet construction.

The district administration's monthly meetings with other motivators, and refresher trainings were very advantageous. They gave us the platform to share the challenges we faced in the field. Collectively, we achieved our dream of making our district 'Open

Defecation Free Tiruvannamalai'. I later received appreciation from the project director for playing a significant role in making our district ODF. Today, I feel empowered as a woman to be in touch with all the district and block officials, including the district collector, whom I update with my assessment of the sanitation status of the district from time to time.

Following our grand achievement, I had a chance to attend the ODF Sustainability training at SIRD. Having started with CAS, I was further introduced to a new concept – Community Based Monitoring Mapping (CBM). Returning to the district, I began to implement CBM, and actively worked on sustaining my district's ODF status.

I gathered a team of around 200 NSS students from Arignar Anna Government Arts College, Cheyyar, and together we created awareness about the importance of safe sanitation at Irungal panchayat of Anakkavur block. On doing a CBM exercise, we would sometimes find toilets that were not in use and needed minor repairs. We improvised our approach then as we moved ahead, placing greater emphasis on the retrofitting of toilets and ensuring that they were used regularly. I would then go door to door, generate awareness and help the household repair their toilets.

During this time my husband, who was very supportive of my journey as a swachhagrahi, passed away. My life felt benighted after this loss; I was distraught, and did not leave my home for months. But not only did my interest for sanitation not fade away, it actually gave me a renewed purpose to start my life all over again. With my mother's and children's support, I resumed my work with an even greater spirit and enthusiasm.

In 2019, during the Swachh Sundar Shauchalaya campaign, my work came to light again. I received an award from the Prime Minister of India as a part of Swachh Shakti 2019 at Kurukshetra in recognition of my efforts. It was a remarkably humbling moment for me personally. I am incredibly grateful to all the officials and my fellow swachhagrahis who motivated this motivator through all the tough the times.

Today, we are at the brink of creating history in the form of an Open Defecation Free India. I am as enthusiastic as ever to continue my work as a swachhagrahi. As time goes by, I believe this is one volunteering position which will always be a part of me. I'd like to end with a quote by Steve Jobs that drove me through my journey: 'If you are working on something that you really care about, you don't have to be pushed. The vision pulls you.'

Darwaza Band toh Bimaari Band

AMITABH BACHCHAN

SBM ambassador

THE ENDURING SUCCESS of the Swachh Bharat Mission (SBM) has reconfirmed an important aspect about campaigns of common public interest – that a positive change in habits is not only an instrument of behavioural reform; it can also be a transforming cultural change. A good habit eventually becomes a customary practice which is then proudly carried forward by successive generations.

One such good habit is the visible commitment to cleanliness achieved by the nationwide Mission. Values are not always those which are associated with skills and virtues; many are also achieved by a common cause, as has been illustrated by SBM. The Mission is not so much a political reform as it is a public cause for everyone's health – a cause of the people, for the people, and by the people. The ordeals and tolls of epidemics are not unknown to most parts of India – like the outbreaks of cholera, typhoid, plague, and many more. It is an honour and privilege to be among those who have wholeheartedly embraced this Mission. There is a pride in raising one's voice in support of a cause which benefits all.

If anyone had suggested to Mahatma Gandhi that the idea of a Swachh Bharat would be a national rage almost a hundred years after his hope, he might perhaps have brushed it aside. But seeing the strides the Mission has made in the past five years, I am certain that if Bapu was with us today, he would have been both surprised and delighted.

Even a few years ago, a movement like SBM may have seemed like a lost cause. The country appeared to be too vast and broken to come together for a common social cause, hardly a place for celebrating the unity of a collective purpose. There were other more exigent miseries to overcome, such as famines, poverty, epidemics and communal disharmony. Yet, now, over seventy years after Independence, the voice of the whole nation has surfaced in unison to support the cause of a Swachh Bharat.

When he addressed the Indian diaspora at Madison Square in New York a month after his landmark announcement for a Swachh Bharat in August 2014, it became clear to resident and non-resident Indians alike that the Mission was an important part of the Prime Minister's vision for the country. And the combined reaction was: 'Yes, we must do this!'

Swachh tann, swachh mann,
Swachh Bharat, mera parichay!

The spontaneous approval and cooperation of the people for SBM will rank among the most unifying events of post-Independence India.

The most inspiring volunteers in the Mission have been the children of schools who actually practise what is preached. The annual day-long 'cleanathon' on 2 October every year has been a revelation in this process. Children of various schools across the country appear on the screen and demonstrate their belief in this Mission with applications of science and technology for cleanliness. If this is an indication, SBM will only grow from strength to strength from here.

Cleaning one beach and a hospital or a patch of forest might only be a symbolic gesture. But cleaning every street and field in every corner of a vast subcontinent is an enormous task. Every citizen who makes it happen deserves to be honoured.

For instance, in a small pilgrimage town, a pick-up truck drives slowly through a lane every morning, ringing a bell. The residents come out of their houses promptly, and put the garbage in the back of the truck. The lane is spotless.

Where there is a toilet in every house of a remote hamlet, men and women do not go into the fields for defecation. The fields do not smell like cesspits any more. The environment is gradually recovering its pristine state as intended by nature.

This is apart from the benefits of health and hygiene. Closed toilets prevent the inception and spread of waterborne and airborne diseases which destroy the ecosystem.

In this sense, SBM is also preserving the quality of the Earth. Open defecation causes irreparable damage to nature, which provides for all. It does not take long for a healthy, productive soil to turn into lifeless sand in an arid desert. In the process of changing habits for the wider objective of saving the ecosystems, the concept of Darwaza Band is a good habit for the health of both the people and the environment.

To this end, the dissemination of the vision and purpose of the Mission was only a first step. SBM did not ask if cleanliness was required. It did not ask who was going to do it. It did not order. It did not coerce anyone. It just made everyone aware that the Mission was on. Everyone was invited. And everyone joined.

Prime Minister Narendra Modi's call to clean the whole nation was not his alone. It was the silent voice of the entire nation. Everyone, from the remotest hamlets in the Himalayas to the wet coasts of Kerala, heard it loud and clear.

Credit is also due to traditional media and social media for taking the Mission across the nation – and making sure that no one is left out. SBM has become a people's movement by virtue of its inherent personal appeal. Everyone went from 'mere dus gaz' to 'mera desh' in one giant leap.

The private and public enterprises which put their might behind the cause, investing efforts, materials, machinery and money without claiming additional perks, deserve recognition as well. This sense of belonging alone can make such an extensive Mission possible and worthwhile.

This jan andolan – the people's movement – has swelled in both size and scope since the launch of the Mission.

Long ago, when Mahatma Gandhi's cry for freedom reached every nook and corner of the subcontinent, the nation rose in resistance.

Today, once again, the nation has risen when the aspiration of a Swachh Bharat has been felt by everyone.

Once again, people have accepted inconvenience for a good cause.

Once again, a humanity of more than a billion people has joined hands.

Once again, each person is assured that they are not alone in their love for nature; a whole nation is with them.

The dignity and prosperity of a nation is founded in such unifying missions. May the Swachh Bharat Mission be the beginning of greater causes of transformation, integrity and higher ideals.

Pro Poor, Pro Women

SURJIT S. BHALLA
Economist

INDIA'S PERFORMANCE IN poverty reduction, since the early 1990s, has been remarkable. However, there is a constant lament that while the decline in consumption poverty has been large, the improvement in social indicators like education and mortality has not been as commendable. Absolute poverty declined from 46 per cent in 1993–94 to only 13 per cent in 2011–12 (Tendulkar poverty line of Rs 27 per capita per day in 2011–12 prices and/or World Bank international poverty line of $1.90 PPP dollars per person per day).

Social indicators showed that in parameters like stunting (height for weight) and wasting (weight for height) India lagged behind the poorer countries of sub-Saharan Africa. To address this anomaly, Indian governments increased the expenditure on food supply, the Right to Food Act, the Right to Education Act, and even the Right to Employment. Similar policies had been in operation in India earlier as well. The Maharashtra food for work programme, for instance, first became operational in 1973. However, while these programmes did make a dent on income poverty to a limited extent, social indicators still lagged behind sub-Saharan Africa.

But there is evidence that India's performance in social indicators is improving, and is now keeping pace with its poverty reduction achievements. Indian policymakers are belatedly recognizing that growth per se brings about an enhancement in living standard indicators, i.e. parents invest more in their child's education when they have more income. Some indicators of welfare belong to what have classically been called public goods (and public bads). As taught in Econ 101, a public good is one that has no exclusion – if it is made available to one person, it is made available to all. A classic example of public good – radio airwaves! Of public bad – air pollution.

While Indian policymakers have provided a multiplicity of private goods to the poor, they have been reluctant to provide genuine public goods. In a 2007 working paper for the Planning Commission, Arvind Virmani pointed out that one important reason for India's poor performance in social indicators was the lack of public goods advancement; in particular, the provision of sanitation. Since 2007, research on Indian sanitation has proved Virmani right. Both academics and policymakers have recognized the importance of sanitation. One of the signature reforms of Prime Minister Narendra Modi, announced from the ramparts of the Red Fort on 15 August 2014, was the Swachh Bharat Mission (SBM). The major goal of this programme was to make India Open Defecation Free (ODF) by 2 October 2019, the 150th birth anniversary of Mahatma Gandhi, the original proponent of a Clean India. Unfortunately, our reformers forgot Gandhi's message as they proceeded to make India modern and prosperous but without considering improvements in sanitation.

Both socially, and politically, the ODF India initiative was a bold one. As a surprise to all, in India and around the world, a word taboo in everyday conversation – 'defecation' – was openly discussed, and by the PM no less. That more than 60 per cent of rural India was indulging in this practice came as a shock to most. This was not what the elite, especially the upper-class elite belonging to the 'in the name of the poor' group, had discussed even in private, let alone in public.

The ODF India campaign has had its fair share of detractors and criticism has moved through three stages. The first stage was close to complete rejection of any possibility of success; 'we have seen this movie before' was the common refrain, and hence, the idea that crores of Indians would change their centuries-old habit was dismissed out of hand. There was evidence to support this dismissal. Incomes in rural areas had increased manifold since Independence in 1947, yet a large proportion of rural Indians were still defecating in the open in 2014. Income change had had almost a zero effect on habits – hence, the conclusion that the Government of India's goal of a defecation-free India by 2019 was a pipe dream.

Nevertheless, the Government persisted with its plan. This brought forth the second round of 'conscientious objectors'. Yes, toilets were being built, but they were being used for storage of grain and for every other purpose imaginable but not as a toilet. Clearly, habits were not being changed. There was evidence in the form of photographs and newspaper interviews with villagers testifying to the non-use of toilets. The results of the first survey of toilet usage (conducted by the Quality Council of India) were published in 2016, and were encouraging. But, and there is always a 'but' in reforming India, the survey was criticized for biased sample selection, i.e. it only surveyed 'high-performing' regions, and hence could not be relied upon as being indicative of what was happening in the backward states of India – such as Bihar – which were not part of the survey.

The third, and partially valid, strand of criticism was that while the toilets had been built, and individuals (especially women) were willing to use them, there was no running water and hence the toilets were white elephants. I had an occasion to test some of these claims (both pros and cons) when I visited a village in the Guna district in Madhya Pradesh in November 2018.

This visit was possibly my most heart-warming experience in my work as a (development) economist. In the dominantly scheduled caste village, I was confronted by six angry young women. They were vocal, and self-assertive (in a very positive way). They were demanding their rights. What rights? Their neighbour had received money to build a toilet (under the auspices of SBM) but they had not. That same neighbour had received money to build a house, but they had not. India has always had subsidies in the name of the poor but, for the first time, I was able to witness these subsidies at work, which explained the loud complaints.

Toilets have been built. In some states, upon geo-tagging the toilet using SBM's app designed for this purpose, Rs 12,000 is deposited into the beneficiary's bank account. But how are poor people going to obtain the few thousand rupees necessary for construction to begin? In some states, an instalment is given up front for economically weaker sections. However, since SBM bases the Rs 12,000 as an incentive, the idea is to motivate the households to invest in the benefits of safe sanitation themselves, regardless of the money. Still, not all deserving people in Indian villages (the bottom 50 per cent) can be first to get their toilets and houses built (costing Rs 2.5 lakh per house and paid by the Government). There is a queue, and those whose turn has not yet come are complaining. Genuine, legitimate complaints. But the same people – and in particular, the same women – are sending their children to school, and proud of the girls doing well in college. And yes, those who have the toilets are using them, especially the women; and are doing so with a water storage tank attached to the toilet, thus debunking the myth that running water is a must for toilet usage.

It may well be that SBM is the most important reform initiative of the Modi Government. How has it performed? What are the statistics about the decline in open defecation in India? How can long entrenched social attitudes change so quickly, especially when 'expert' studies have shown that this is a long and arduous journey which barely started four years ago? Some assert that Government statistics do not help because they are *Government* statistics, and hence, not that credible.

International Evidence on ODF

Since 2000, the World Bank has been reporting data on open defecation (OD) for more than 120 countries (urban and rural). This is a rich source of data to examine the performance of SBM. Data are available from 2000 when India is reported to have 82.2 per cent of rural population practicing OD; 62.7 per cent in 2011; and 57.4 and 55.6 per cent in 2014 and 2015, respectively.

Census reports rural OD as 78 per cent and 67 per cent in 2001 and 2011 respectively; Government of India statistics for 2014 and 2015 are reported as 61 per cent and 55 per cent. In other words, GoI data, census data and World Bank data are near identical.

The best three-year performance in the decline in OD among 108 countries since 2000 was in Ethiopia – a decline of 11.5 percentage points (ppt) between 2004 (74.3 per cent) and 2007 (62.8 per cent). The second and third best performers were Cambodia (-8.3 per cent) and Pakistan (-8 per cent). At seventh place was neighbouring Nepal and India was ranked thirteenth. One important note about these data: the pace of decline is reported linearly for each individual country. For example, between 2000 and 2003, rural OD in India declined from 82.2 per cent to 76.9 per cent, a decline of 5.3 ppt; between 2012 and 2015 the decline was the same – from 60.9 per cent to 55.6 per cent.

In 2018, the Government of India's website reports a rural OD magnitude of 8.8 per cent. This means that no matter how you slice the data (and even assuming some 11 ppt overstatement in the GoI figures, i.e. rural OD was 20 per cent in 2018 rather than the reported 9 per cent) the decline over three years in OD is a staggering 35.6 ppt (from 55.6 per cent in 2015 to 20 per cent in 2018). This is more than three times the best-ever observed in the world, at least since comparable data first became available in 2000. It might be worth researching the best three-year performance for all the countries in the world since the invention of the toilet circa 1852. Note that this record performance in India would still occur even if the Government is vastly overstating the achievement of SBM – even if OD in 2018 was five times the OD figure of 8.8 per cent i.e. 44 per cent, it would still be a world record.

But there is more to the Swachh Bharat policy achievement. The World Bank publishes annual data for more than 180 countries on several living-standard indicators. These data (on mortality rates for infants and children under five) can provide some indication about the pace of improvement in India post the introduction of SBM, say from 2014 onwards (with 2014 as the cut-off year for before the Mission). The mortality data are being looked at because apart from safety and dignity for women, open defecation has major implications for mortality, and especially mortality rates for children. If ODF India has been even partially successful, it should show up in mortality rates for small children (under the age of five). Note that looking at the pace of mortality reduction is not a very stringent test for the success/failure of the ODF programme.

It is not a strict test because mortality decline is affected by at least four other important factors – income growth, technological advances (medicine and vaccination), improvement in water supply, and education of women. All of these indicators are improving in India, so one cannot attribute the reduction in infant or under-five mortality to the reduction in OD alone. Possibly, becoming ODF is the most important, but how does one prove it?

The first goal is to compare like with like, i.e. compare India to its peers, loosely defined as emerging economies (aka developing countries) with a population greater than five million. Second is to rank their performance, with top rank for the country with the fastest rate of decline.

One possible method is to look at the pace of decline of mortality indicators. But there are several international factors (advancement in medicines, technology, etc.) that can increase the pace of mortality decline in India. Hence, looking at *just* the changes in the speed of change may not be that meaningful. There is one method, however, that can 'isolate' the country-specific trend from international trend influences. It is to look at the *rank* of the speed of change i.e. if India's pace of change is greater than its comparators, then that can be indicative of some domestic policy factor.

Out of a sample of sixty-five developing non-oil exporting economies with a population greater than, or equal to, five million,

India, in 2014, showed the thirteenth fastest decline in infant mortality rates, and the eleventh fastest decline in under-five mortality rates. Three years later, in 2017, the ranks had improved to seventh and sixth respectively.

One must give credit where credit is due. Academics said such a fast rate of change was not possible. Well-known bureaucratic inertia in India meant that even if theoretically (academically) possible, implementation of the ODF campaign would face insurmountable hurdles.

Why did the programme succeed beyond all calculations? Because it was a pro-poor, pro-women campaign. Because it improved the safety and dignity of women. Because it was (shockingly!) very well administered. And because it was a high-profile PM-led campaign.

Chalo Champaran

TAVLEEN SINGH

Journalist

Ten years ago when I moved to the seaside village in Maharashtra where I now live, the one thing I hated was that everyone defecated on the beach. In the mornings, when I went jogging, I would see long lines of women squatting wherever there were patches of wild beach shrubs. When they saw me in my jogging shorts they would giggle and point to my naked legs, seemingly unaware that they were exposing far more than me. Open defecation was socially acceptable. So the village ladies behaved as if they were at a kitty party. They gossiped and giggled and did not mind when tourists stared in horror.

Women defecated, mostly, in the early hours of the morning. Men defecated at all times and anywhere. When the tide was out they squatted on the wet, soggy parts of the beach where the water had receded so that sea water spared them the bother of bringing water with them. There was no escaping the defecators. Not at sunrise and not at sunset. The stench of human excrement so filled the air that I gave up going to the beach. When friends came to visit I warned them to not even think about lying on the beach or bathing in the sea. When the Prime Minister announced from the ramparts of the Red Fort his determination to end the practice of open defecation, I cheered but did not expect him to succeed.

Then because of something critical I wrote about the Swachh Bharat Mission (SBM) I met Parameswaran Iyer. We met in the Gymkhana Club in Delhi. He introduced himself as Secretary in the Ministry of Water and Sanitation and I think the first thing he said was that I was wrong in saying that the Mission was failing. We ordered eggs – poached for me and an omelette for him – and hot buttery toast and 'desi' chai. But, our entire conversation at this very wholesome breakfast was about open defecation in rural India.

I think I said that sanitation was not possible unless there was water and this was scarce in most Indian villages. So he described in detail the twin-pit toilets that they were building which use very little water. When one pit gets filled, he said, it is closed and the other brought into use. In a year the closed pit is transformed into a goldmine of manure. Some days later a newspaper printed a photograph of this tall, refined man standing in a pit running this 'gold' through his fingers. I was impressed with his disdain for caste taboos, his passion and his perseverance.

At one of our other meetings, he told me that my village was now 'ODF' (Open Defecation Free). I did not believe this possible and conducted my own survey. It astounded me to discover that every house in the village now had a private toilet. These had been built with the subsidies the Government offered under SBM. The beach is now so ODF that it has become a low-budget tourist's dream. There are tiny restaurants now, coconut stands, jet-skis for hire and horse riding. I became more interested in the Mission and on my rural travels made it a point to ask wherever I went about sanitation. When I came upon a village where open defecation prevailed I reported it to the Secretary.

In early 2018, at one of our breakfast meetings, he told me that the Prime Minister was coming to Champaran to meet SBM volunteers, swachhagrahis. Champaran was chosen because it was where the Mahatma had started his Satyagraha movement. 'Satyagraha Se Swachhagraha' was the theme of this conference, he said, and they were expecting thousands of young volunteers to come to Champaran. I said I would love to come if he could promise me a clean toilet. The irony of asking the man in charge of SBM for a clean lavatory made us both laugh. But, decades of covering rural India have left me with a deep horror of dirty toilets.

When I arrived in Champaran on a balmy April evening, the first thing I checked was if my room in the SS Exotica Hotel did indeed have a clean toilet. And, then I wandered towards the vast tented city that had been set up for the swachhagrahis. On the way I saw hundreds of young men and women wearing white jackets and white Gandhi caps and recognized them as the army of sanitation volunteers that SBM has created. In the tented city, I met young girls and boys, who had never left their village before, who told me proudly that they were teaching elders in their village about the importance of ending open defecation.

When I asked how they did this they gave me examples. 'We put a hair on a pile of shit, then dip it into a glass of water and ask them to drink it. When they refuse we ask them to think how much dirtier their food is when flies who have six legs sit on it after they have sat on human excrement.' Another example that seemed to have great impact was telling open defecators that the number of Indian children who died every day due to lack of sanitation would fill two jumbo jets.

The more than 20,000 volunteers in this small tented township had come from all over India. They had been inspired to travel to Champaran because they had heard that Bihar was one of the states lagging behind when it came to SBM. They wanted to inspire the Bihari populace to join the movement.

When the Prime Minister arrived the next day he was visibly moved. 'Prime Ministers are not born with a thousand hands,' he said, 'but now I know that you young people have given me a thousand hands.' He made special mention of Param Iyer and said the movement may not have taken off in the way it had if Param had not played such a key role. I saw my breakfast companion seated quietly in the audience looking more than a little embarrassed. But I second what the Prime Minister said.

Leadership can make all the difference when it comes to a movement like SBM. It was this dedication and the Prime Minister's passionate support that has made it possible for us to imagine a time when it can no longer be said of Indians what the writer V.S. Naipaul so cruelly did in his book *An Area of Darkness*: 'Indians defecate everywhere. They defecate, mostly, beside the railway tracks. But they also defecate on the river banks; they defecate on the streets; they never look for cover.'

These words were written fifty years ago and would probably be true fifty years from now if Narendra Modi had not dared to declare, in an Independence Day speech from the Red Fort, that it was time for open defecation to stop. The Swachh Bharat Mission will be remembered as one of the most important achievements of his first tenure as the Prime Minister of India.

Epilogue

PARAMESWARAN IYER

THE SWACHH BHARAT Mission (SBM) has become a leading example for participatory development. It has shown that transformative change can be achieved if every person contributes to and becomes a part of the revolution. From recruiting lakhs of swachhagrahis to spread the message of sanitation, to helping thousands of rani mistris break gender stereotypes and construct toilets, to having the Swachh Bharat logo on every new currency note in the country – SBM went far beyond the mandate of just one Ministry.

SBM endeavoured to practise what Richard Thaler, the 2017 Nobel Prize-winning economist, preached on behavioural economics and, in particular, on the art of 'nudging' – how small interventions help individuals or communities change deep-seated behaviours. Over the last five years SBM has been, perhaps at a scale unimaginable to Thaler, nudging rural communities in India to change their habit of open defecation by using household toilets. These gentle nudges have come through with massive returns.

SBM has had a positive impact on the life, health, wealth and dignity of rural communities. These have been well documented and spoken about. Amplifying these benefits is SBM's impact on the market economy and, in particular, on job creation, which is significant by itself. The massive improvement in India's sanitation coverage has resulted in direct employment opportunities for masons, labourers and industries involved in supplying sanitaryware, and indirect opportunities for several associated sectors. One toilet needs on an average one mason and two labourers to work for three days, meaning the construction of one toilet requires an average of nine person-days of work. For the construction of 9.7 crore toilets (progress as of June 2019) under SBM-Grameen, an estimated 87 crore person-days of employment have been generated. Assuming that one person-year of work comprises 200 working days, these total to well over 40 lakh person-years of work!

SBM has contributed significantly to the country's future productivity. UNICEF had earlier estimated that nearly 38 per cent of India's children under five were physically and cognitively stunted, primarily because of the lack of sanitation. The inability of such a large portion of our future workforce to reach their full productive capacity poses a serious threat to our biggest strength – our demographic dividend. SBM's impact on reducing malnutrition had been studied through the Bill & Melinda Gates Foundation health impact study which found that in Open Defecation Free (ODF) areas, there were 32 per cent fewer cases of diarrhoea among children, 15 per cent fewer cases of stunting, and 32 per cent fewer cases of women with below normal BMI. Better nutrition and better health for women and children directly contribute to higher school attendance and improved learning outcomes.

What the last five years have proved beyond doubt is the importance of collective action when it comes to public health. The rapid improvements in sanitation across the country have had a positive spin-off on various other sectors of development as well. The effectiveness of other flagship programmes of the Government like Integrated Child Development Services, Skill India, Beti Bachao Beti Padhao and Make in India, among others, has increased manifold simply by improving the nutrition intake capacity of children and improving overall productivity.

Becoming everyone's business, SBM set itself at the centre of the national discourse, comfortably making its way into everyone's consciousness. Compared to pre-2014, every citizen of the country is much more aware today about the once shunned topic of open defecation and toilets. The 2019 study by BMGF on the assessment of SBM's behaviour change communication gave us a number to put that in context: since 2014, the average rural Indian was reached by SBM messaging over 3,000 times. That's almost twice a day every day for four and a half years!

Making a village free from open defecation is not a one-time activity, but a continuous process. SBM continues to focus on communication for ODF Sustainability. All villages are constantly reminded by swachhagrahis that they must not let the ball drop on sanitation. Nigrani samitis will continue to be in place until using a toilet becomes second nature. Mass media campaigns featuring celebrities serve as a reminder of the benefits of using a toilet every day through punch lines like 'Har Koi, Har Roz, Hamesha' – 'Everyone, Every day, Always'. And with our country's children leading the way in the sanitation revolution, the future is promising.

As implementers, however, we have to get the right tools in place in a timely manner. For the most part, the idea is to achieve and sustain holistic sanitation and create institutional memory to take sanitation into account for years to come. With the country on the brink of becoming ODF, the Mission is focusing heavily on its sustainability even as it actively moves to the next level – ODF Plus.

ODF Plus is the broader goal of overall cleanliness in India's villages. The key factors in becoming ODF Plus are ODF-Sustainability, Solid Waste Management (biodegradable and non-biodegradable) and Liquid Waste Management (Grey Water and Faecal Sludge Management), as required. A village would be considered ODF Plus if it continues to sustain its ODF status and safely manages its solid and liquid waste. We are committed to ensuring that every village moves from ODF to ODF Plus over the next few years.

To reorient and institutionalize the capacities of members of panchayati raj institutions and swachhagrahis towards ODF Plus, a pool of skilled field trainers is being created in every district. These trainers will further build the capabilities of around 11 lakh village-level functionaries (beginning with 2.5 lakh sarpanchs, 2.5 lakh panchayat secretaries, about 6 lakh swachhagrahis and masons) with adequate information and knowledge on keeping the sanitation momentum soaring ahead, and moving from ODF to ODF Plus.

One thing is for sure – the change is real, and the change is here. As we end this book, the first chapter of the next era of sanitation is already taking shape. The Government of India has taken a momentous step towards an integrated take on water resources management and sanitation in the country by creating a new Ministry – the Ministry of Jal Shakti. With the merging of the Ministry of Water Resources, River Development and Ganga Rejuvenation and the Ministry of Drinking Water and Sanitation, the stage is set for an integrated approach to managing water more efficiently, preventing its wastage and maximizing its utility. This Ministry will work towards bringing *Har Ghar Nal Se Jal* (piped water supply to all households) by 2024, with mandatory source sustainability and grey water reuse and recharge measures for an integrated and holistic approach to water and sanitation under the Jal Jeevan Mission. This ambitious programme is also intended to become a jan andolan, a people's movement like the SBM.

On 15 August 2014, we witnessed a defining moment in India's modern history – a tipping point which led the country to a revolution. SBM is a fascinating story of the power of the collective and a successful model that other national and international programmes can learn from. It is a shot in the arm for the world striving to achieve the Sustainable Development Goals. But most of all, it is a story of what is possible if one inspired man makes an earnest appeal to a nation and challenges his people to achieve something which no one thought was achievable.

References

1. 'The Economic Impacts of Inadequate Sanitation in India', Water and Sanitation Program, World Bank, New Delhi, https://www.wsp.org/sites/wsp/files/publications/wsp-esi-india.pdf (2006).
2. 'An assessment of the reach and value of IEC activities under Swachh Bharat Mission (Grameen)', Department of Drinking Water and Sanitation, Ministry of Jal Shakti, Government of India, New Delhi, https://jalshakti-ddws.gov.in/sites/default/files/201906_SBM_IEC_Whitepaper.pdf (2019).
3. 'The Sanitation Economy in India: Market Estimates and Insights', Toilet Board Coalition, Geneva, https://www.toiletboard.org/media/35-The_Sanitation_Economy_in_India.pdf (2017).
4. 'National Annual Rural Sanitation Survey (NARSS) 2017-18'.
5. 'National Annual Rural Sanitation Survey (NARSS) 2018-19'.
6. 'Sustainable Development Goals', Sustainable Development Goals Knowledge Platform, United Nations, New York, https://sustainabledevelopment.un.org/?menu=1300.
7. 'Swachhagrahi Guidelines, Ministry of Drinking Water and Sanitation, Government of India, New Delhi, https://jalshakti-ddws.gov.in/sites/default/files/Swachhagrahi_Guidelines_2018.pdf (2018).

8. 'The Future of World Religions: Population Growth Projections, 2010-2050', PEW Research Center, Washington, https://www.pewforum.org/2015/04/02/religious-projections-2010-2050/.
9. 'Census of India 2001', Office of the Registrar General & Census Commissioner, Ministry of Home Affairs, Government of India, New Delhi, http://censusindia.gov.in/Census_And_You/religion.aspx.
10. Aditi Malhotra, '5 Things Mahatma Gandhi Said About Sanitation', *The Wall Street Journal*, New York, https://blogs.wsj.com/briefly/2015/10/01/5-things-mahatma-gandhi-said-about-sanitation/ (1 October 2015).
11. Nauzer Bharucha, 'Mumbai dumps 2,100mn litres of human waste in sea daily', *The Times of India*, Mumbai, https://timesofindia.indiatimes.com/city/mumbai/mumbai-dumps-2100mn-litres-of-human-waste-in-sea-daily/articleshow/58676358.cms (15 May 2017).
12. 'Global Digital Report 2018', We Are Social, New York, https://digitalreport.wearesocial.com/ (2018).
13. 'Financial and Economic Impacts of the Swachh Bharat Mission in India', UNICEF, New Delhi, http://unicef.in/Uploads/Publications/Resources/pub_doc20172.PDF (2018).
14. 'People practicing open defecation, rural', World Bank, Washington, https://data.worldbank.org/indicator/SH.STA.ODFC.RU.ZS?end=2000&locations=IN&start=2000&view=bar (2015).
15. Arvind Virmani, 'The Sudoku of Growth, Poverty and Malnutrition: Policy Implications for Lagging States', Working Paper, Planning Commission, New Delhi, http://www.planningcommission.gov.in/reports/wrkpapers/wp07StJl12.pdf (2007).
16. N. Ashraf, E.L. Glaeser and G.A. Ponzetto, 'Infrastructure, Incentives, and Institutions', *American Economic Review*, 106

(5), pp. 77-82, https://www.aeaweb.org/articles?id=10.1257/aer.p20161095 (2016).

17. Roberta V. Gatti, A.C. Kraay, C. Avitabile, M. Collin, R. Dsouza and N. Dehnen, 'The Human Capital Project', World Bank Group, Washington, http://documents.worldbank.org/curated/en/363661540826242921/pdf/131462-PublicHCPReportCompleteBooklet.pdf (2018).
18. A.J. Pickering, H. Djebbari, C. Lopez, M. Coulibaly and M.L. Alzua, 'Effect of a Community-Led Sanitation Intervention on Child Diarrhoea and Child Growth in Rural Mali: A Cluster-Randomised Controlled Trial', *Lancet Global Health* 3 (5), E701–11, https://www.thelancet.com/journals/langlo/article/PIIS2214-109X(15)00144-8/fulltext (2015).
19. 'Women's Leadership in SBM-Grameen', Ministry of Drinking Water and Sanitation, Government of India, New Delhi, http://swachhsangraha.gov.in/sites/default/files/WB_Women%27s_Leadership_Report_English_1.pdf (2018).

Index

About the Contributors

Raghubar Das is the Chief Minister of Jharkhand. He was sworn in as the sixth Chief Minister of the state in December 2014.

Kevin Rudd is the Chair, Sanitation and Water for All. He was the twenty-sixth Prime Minister of Australia, serving from December 2007 to June 2010 and again from June to September 2013.

Uma Bharti was the Union Minister of the erstwhile Ministry of Drinking Water and Sanitation from September 2017 to May 2019.

Rajiv Mehrishi is the Comptroller and Auditor General of India (CAG) and Vice-Chairman of the United Nations Panel of External Auditors. He is a retired 1978 batch IAS officer.

Arun Baroka is the Additional Secretary, Department of Drinking Water and Sanitation, Ministry of Jal Shakti. He is a 1990 batch IAS officer.

Professor Valerie Curtis is Director of the Environmental Health Group at the London School of Hygiene and Tropical Medicine.

Priyanka Shukla is a 2009 batch IAS officer, who implemented the Swachh Bharat Mission-Grameen in Jashpur district of Chhattisgarh.

Suleiman H. Adamu is the Minister of Water Resources, Government of Nigeria. He assumed office in November 2015.

Arun Jaitley is a former Union Minister of Finance, Government of India. He held the office from May 2014 to May 2019.

Cheryl Hicks is the Executive Director and CEO of the Toilet Board Coalition, a global, business-led coalition of leading companies, social investors, sanitation experts and non-profit organizations.

Hartwig Schafer is the World Bank's Vice President for the South Asia region and leads the Bank's relations with Afghanistan, Bangladesh, Bhutan, India, Maldives, Nepal, Pakistan, and Sri Lanka.

Guy Hutton is a development economist, currently serving as Senior Advisor, UNICEF. He has twenty-five years of experience in the fields of water, sanitation, health, air pollution and climate change.

Nicolas Osbert is Chief, Water, Sanitation, Hygiene (WASH), at UNICEF India. He has twenty years of experience in WASH and Public Health in Africa, Latin America and Asia.

Francis Odhiambo is Chief, WASH, at UNICEF Tanzania, where he has the overall responsibility for the planning and delivery of the WASH programme of assistance to the Government of Tanzania.

Bindeshwar Pathak is an Indian sociologist and the founder of Sulabh International, a social service organization which works to promote human rights, environmental sanitation, non-conventional sources of energy, waste management and social reforms.

Gary White is a co-founder of Water.org and WaterEquity, non-profit organizations dedicated to solving the global water and sanitation crisis.

Matt Damon is a co-founder of Water.org and WaterEquity, non-profit organizations dedicated to solving the global water and sanitation crisis.

Amitabh Kant is a 1980 batch IAS officer. He is the CEO of NITI Aayog, a policy think tank of the Government of India.

Arvind Panagariya is Professor of Economics and Jagdish Bhagwati Professor of Indian Political Economy at Columbia University, New York.

Adil Zainulbhai is the Chairman of Quality Council of India, the apex Quality Body in India under the Ministry of Commerce and Industry.

Akshay Rout has various teams focused on IEC at the erstwhile Ministry of Drinking Water and Sanitation since 2016.

Naina Lal Kidwai is the Chair of the India Sanitation Coalition. She was formerly President of the Federation of Indian Chambers of Commerce and Industry (FICCI).

Ratan N. Tata is the Chairman of Tata Trusts, one of India's oldest and largest non-sectarian philanthropic organizations.

Mahima Vashisht is as a consultant at the office of the Secretary, Department of Drinking Water and Sanitation, Ministry of Jal Shakti, on deputation from the Tata Trusts.

Vineet Jain is a consultant at the office of the Secretary, Department of Drinking Water and Sanitation, Ministry of Jal Shakti, on deputation from the Tata Trusts.

Karishma Kadyan is a consultant at the office of the Secretary, Department of Drinking Water and Sanitation, Ministry of Jal Shakti, on deputation from the Tata Trusts.

Sanjay Gupta is a Director at Jagran Prakashan Ltd and CEO and Editor in Chief of *Dainik Jagran*, India's leading daily newspaper in Hindi. He has more than thirty-one years of experience in the print media industry.

Sadhvi Bhagawati Saraswati is the Secretary General of the Global Interfaith WASH Alliance (GIWA), an initiative launched by UNICEF, in partnership with the governments of the United States of America and the Netherlands.

Sadhguru is the Founder of Isha Foundation, a non-religious, non-profit, public service organization, which works on overall human wellbeing through its Yoga and Outreach programmes.

Vijay Kiran Anand is a 2009 batch IAS officer. He was previously the Mission Director, Swachh Bharat Mission-Grameen, Uttar Pradesh, and Mela Adhikari for the Kumbh Mela 2019.

Neeta Verma is the Director General of National Informatics Centre (NIC), the premier ICT organization of the Government of India.

Deepak Chandra Misra is a scientist 'G'/DDG level of officer at NIC, MeitY, Government of India.

Seemantinee Sengupta is a scientist 'F' level of officer at NIC, MeitY, Government of India.

Akshay Kumar is a Hindi film actor and has been a leading brand ambassador for the Swachh Bharat Mission-Grameen since the release of his film *Toilet: Ek Prem Katha*.

Mark Suzman is the Chief Strategy Officer and President, Bill & Melinda Gates Foundation. He manages foundation-wide learning initiatives and critical strategic trade-offs across all the foundation's work.

Henrietta H. Fore is the Executive Director of the United Nations Children's Fund. She has worked to champion economic development, education, health, humanitarian assistance and disaster relief in a public service, private sector and non-profit leadership career that spans more than four decades.

P.K. Sinha served as the thirty-first Cabinet Secretary of India from 2015 to 2019. He is a 1977 batch IAS officer from the Uttar Pradesh cadre.

Bibek Debroy is an Indian economist and Chairperson of the Prime Minister's Economic Advisory Council (PMEAC).

Radhika Sundaramoorty is a swachhagrahi from the Tiruvannamalai district of Tamil Nadu. She played a key role in making her district Open Defecation Free through her behaviour change efforts.

Amitabh Bachchan is a Hindi film actor who has been the most prominent national brand ambassador of the Swachh Bharat Mission-Grameen. He has been the face of many Swachh Bharat campaigns including SBM's flagship campaign – Darwaza Band (close the door to open defecation).

Surjit S. Bhalla is a leading Indian economist who has served on several committees of the Government of India as an advisor.

Tavleen Singh is an Indian columnist, political reporter and writer. She writes regularly for the English daily *Indian Express* and the Hindi daily *Amar Ujala*.

About the Editor

Parameswaran Iyer is Secretary, Department of Drinking Water and Sanitation, Ministry of Jal Shakti – the ministry overseeing the implementation of the flagship Swachh Bharat Mission and the new Jal Jeevan Mission, aimed at providing drinking water to all rural households in India. Prior to his current appointment, Iyer served as Manager for Water in the World Bank based in Washington DC. A former IAS officer, he headed the innovative community-led Swajal Project in Uttar Pradesh and Uttarakhand in the 1990s, and has over 25 years of global experience in the water and sanitation sector, particularly in Vietnam, China, Egypt and Lebanon.

About the Editor

Rural sanitation coverage has increased exponentially, with India becoming Open Defecation Free in October 2019